MW01414702

A Gift For

From

Copyright © 2016 by the estate of Heather McManamy
Sourcebooks and the colophon are registered trademarks of Sourcebooks, Inc.

The photographs found on the following pages are © Jeff McManamy: 9, 14, 48, 68, 82, 90, 96, 104, 112, 117, 136, 137, 143, 149, 158
The photographs found on the following pages are © the estate of Heather McManamy: 17, 20, 22, 38, 39, 52, 58, 64, 67, 76 The photograph found on page 26 is © Laura Frazier/Raspberry Lane Photography
The photograph found on page 28 is © Hillary Schave/Azena Photography
The photograph found on page 34 is © Kate Westaby
The photographs found on pages 41 and 93 are © Kelli Grashel
The photograph found on page 61 is © Brian Joyce
The photograph found on page 86 is © John Grant Photography
The photograph found on page 106 is © Jen Dickman
The photograph found on page 119 is © Katy Morgan-Davies
The photograph found on page 131 is © Scott Jens
All photographs are reprinted with permission of the copyright holders.

"Keg on My Coffin" written by Chris Trapper. Lyrics reprinted with permission from Always Gone Music (SESAC).

This book is not intended as a substitute for medical advice from a qualified physician. The intent of this book is to provide accurate general information in regard to the subject matter covered. If medical advice or other expert help is needed, the services of an appropriate medical professional should be sought.

This book is a memoir. It reflects the author's present recollections of experiences over a period of time. Some names and characteristics have been changed, some events have been compressed, and some dialogue has been re-created.

All brand names and product names used in this book are trademarks, registered trademarks, or trade names of their respective holders. Sourcebooks, Inc., is not associated with any product or vendor in this book.

This edition published in 2016 by Hallmark Gift Books, a division of Hallmark Cards, Inc., Kansas City, MO 64141 under license from Sourcebooks.
Visit us on the Web at Hallmark.com.

All rights reserved. No part of this publication may be reproduced, transmitted, or stored in any form or by any means without the prior written permission of the publisher.

ISBN: 978-1-63059-917-1
BOK1054

Made in China
0916

Cards for Brianna

A Mom's Messages of Living, Laughing, and Loving as Time Is Running Out

By Heather McManamy with William Croyle

Hallmark

Contents

INTRODUCTION	6
CHAPTER 1: TO EXPERIENCE IS TO LIVE	
For Brianna's Retirement	13
CHAPTER 2: LEAVING LOVE IN GOOD HANDS	
When Brianna Gets Her Driver's License	19
CHAPTER 3: LAUGHTER IS THE BEST MEDICINE	
When Brianna is Having a Rough Day	25
CHAPTER 4: ACCEPTING HELP	
A Get-Well Card When Brianna is Sick	31
CHAPTER 5: EVERYTHING WILL BE OKAY	
Brianna's First Day of Elementary School	37
CHAPTER 6: GIVE IT YOUR BEST SHOT	
A "Kick Some Butt" Card During Difficult Times	45
CHAPTER 7: JUST DO IT	
Encouragement in Adulthood	55
CHAPTER 8: DON'T REGRET NOT TRYING	
A "You Can Do It!" Card	63
CHAPTER 9: COMFORT IN, DUMP OUT	
Brianna's Thirteenth Birthday	71
CHAPTER 10: TAKE A BREAK FROM LIFE	
For a Relationship Breakup or Just a Bad Day	79

CHAPTER 11: MOURN AS YOU SEE FIT
The Death of a Pet 89

CHAPTER 12: JUST BE YOURSELF
Brianna's Sixteenth Birthday 95

CHAPTER 13: DANCE ON A BAR SOMEWHERE
Brianna's Twenty-First Birthday 103

CHAPTER 14: SOAK IN THE LOVE
Brianna's Wedding Shower 109

CHAPTER 15: SAY "I LIVED"
Brianna's First Drink with Her Dad 115

CHAPTER 16: TRUE LOVE
Brianna's Wedding 125

CHAPTER 17: EXPLAINING THE UNEXPLAINABLE
Brianna's Eighteenth Birthday 133

CHAPTER 18: FOLLOW YOUR HEART
When Brianna Starts High School 141

EPILOGUE: EVERY DAY MATTERS
Heather's Final Goodbye 155

ACKNOWLEDGMENTS 161

RESOURCES 164

ABOUT THE AUTHORS 166

Introduction

I loved my life. It was perfect. I was a thirty-three-year-old wife to a wonderful husband and the mother of the most beautiful little girl in the world. I had a job that I absolutely loved. We had a modest, comfortable home. Seriously, for a girl from the old working-class Milwaukee suburb of West Allis, Wisconsin—"Stallis," as we called it—I was living a dream.

But then, one evening, a bomb went off: I was lying in bed and felt a lump on my chest.

"What the hell is that?" I exclaimed to Jeff as I popped my head up. Neither of us had ever noticed it. How long had it been there? I spent the rest of the night Googling "lump on chest," trying to find any link that didn't have the word "cancer" in it.

I went to the doctor the next day; that's when the wheels started to come off. I was diagnosed with stage II breast cancer. Less than four weeks later, I had a double mastectomy. I followed that with chemo for more than a year, but it didn't work. The cancer had spread to my bones and liver. I was diagnosed as stage IV terminal, given two years at most to live.

About fourteen months after that terminal diagnosis, I was told the chemo drug I had been taking the past four months to extend my life as much as possible had been outsmarted by the cancer, bringing me a giant leap closer to my inevitable death. This was no surprise. It was my ninth different chemo, and the more that fail, the less likely subsequent ones are to work. Cancer cells eventually mutate and figure out a way to survive, and then the "smart" cells blast through your body like world-class sprinters in a hundred-meter dash. You hope you have a dumb cancer that takes a long time to determine how to get around the chemo. My cancer has proven to be very, very intelligent.

When my oncologist told me that I was terminal, he bluntly warned me what I was in for. "It'll be one heck of a roller coaster ride," he said. "You'll receive bad news after bad news after bad news. You just need to hang on tight for as long as you can."

I'm still hanging on, though sometimes down the big hills, I boldly let go and thrust my hands high into the air . . . because life's just more awesome that way.

As I've reflected on this wild ride of nearly three years, what has struck me most is that no matter how many bombs the cancer has dropped on me during its relentless, take-no-prisoners assault, the world has kept turning. I noticed it instantly when I went from living a "normal" life to being diagnosed and having a double mastectomy in less than a month. I was crashing and burning, yet everything and everyone around me continued moving forward. I still had deadlines at work.

Bills still had to be paid. Laundry still needed to be done. My favorite TV shows kept churning out new episodes. My daughter, Brianna, and husband, Jeff, still needed me. And so, being the stubborn person I am, I decided if I ever had the chance to gain control over anything, I was going to seize it.

I powered through and got my butt out of bed when Bri called out in the middle of the night, even when I was ghastly sick from chemo. I stayed the course and hosted Bri's long-planned birthday party just days prior to my surgery. It was a Yo Gabba Gabba theme held at our home with every rambunctious two-year-old in the state of Wisconsin. As screaming toddlers strung out on sugar gleefully bounced off the walls of our house, a huge piece of me wanted to cower in the corner with fear, not knowing if it would be the last of Bri's birthdays I'd ever celebrate with her—but I couldn't do it. I guess that's what Christopher Robin meant when he so eloquently said to Winnie the Pooh, "Promise me you'll always remember: You're braver than you believe, and stronger than you seem, and smarter than you think." Even though life can be painfully unfair, sometimes you have the ability to fight through adversity and take back a bit of control. And in those moments when I physically couldn't take control of anything, I learned to forgive myself and turn off that critical, nasty voice in my head.

Being confronted with your mortality is hard. So hard. But by accepting the randomness of life and the possibility that anyone could be eaten by a bear tomorrow, one can gain appreciation for the tiniest things most people take for granted. I never would have thought I'd be the type to get up early to watch the sunrise. As cheesy and cliché as that sounds, it makes me sad to think that without cancer, I never would have taken the time to immerse myself in something so captivating. I can't tell you how often I cringe when I watch other people explode in anger because the line at the grocery store is too slow, a red light is taking too long to change to green, or their smartphone isn't working. If only they knew how quickly the bald mom observing them would be willing to swap grievances. I don't always assume I

have it worse than others, but oh, how I want to give reality checks sometimes.

Another lesson I've learned during this ride, one I've shared multiple times with Bri, is how important it is to be kind to others. Just be nice. It's so simple, yet so many people don't do it. I'm astonished at how people's behaviors completely transform when they find out I'm dying. Why couldn't they treat me with such consideration before they knew? Everyone has their own crap in life—illnesses, financial difficulties, chronic conditions, horrible things that happen—whether it's obvious to the world or not. We all have a story, one that may have started many chapters ago and is far from being finished. Being kind to others without judgment will guarantee that you won't stick your foot in your mouth, and more importantly, you might brighten someone's day.

I will say, though, that for as many ignorant and awkward comments as I've received from store cashiers about the photo on my driver's license not matching the hairless woman standing before them ("I see you're going for a new look!"), I've also had people sincerely ask about or recognize my situation and remark that their friend is going through chemo or a family member has been diagnosed with cancer. And you know what? They just want to talk. They want to know how they can help that person they care about. They want to know how to say and do the right things.

Being genuinely open with my situation has resulted in countless people pouring their hearts out to me, including many strangers from around the world, which is pretty beautiful. When I posted on Facebook that I had bought and filled out greeting cards for Bri that would cover the rest of her life, it was meant for my friends and family to cherish. I thought it was something cool within my own world. I never imagined someone in the media would see it, or even care. Then, when a friend told me to Google "dying mom" and I found my story front and center in major publications worldwide, many in languages I didn't understand, I knew I had one more purpose to serve.

Cards for Brianna is my final creation, written from deep within my heart during the last weeks of my life as a gift for Bri, Jeff, friends, family . . . and you. I don't know exactly how long I have remaining, but it was nearly eighteen months ago that I was given that two-year guesstimate. Today, my failing body is telling me that was a fairly accurate prediction and that my time is almost up.

Yes, that sucks in many ways.

But you know what? It's okay. It really is.

As much as I hate cancer with every cell in my body that it hasn't killed yet, this disease has taught me the value of living, laughing, and loving each second I have before this ride comes to a complete stop. I hope *Cards for Brianna* reflects that philosophy and that it's as powerful for you to read as it was for me to write. I also hope, as your world continues to turn, that this book makes you smile at all of your good fortunes, helps you empathize with those who could use a little empathy, and teaches you to live—I mean truly live—each day you have left.

Chapter 1

"I retired because the cancer forced me to. Hopefully you're retiring under better circumstances. Enjoy the heck out of life. Follow your happiness, appreciate each day, and laugh at all the suckers still going to work. And I hope your coworkers gave you a great party."

—for Brianna's retirement in (hopefully) fifty or sixty years

To Experience Is to Live
For Brianna's Retirement

At my retirement party, about a month after finding out my days were numbered, I did what any dying, depressed, recently unemployed mom would do: I hopped on a ferocious mechanical bull named Red Rock, and I rode him longer than anyone else in the bar could. A week later, I went to the hospital for a bone scan, and my spine lit up with cancer. It had likely been there for a while, but previous scans hadn't picked it up.

"Sooo . . . was riding a bull last week not a good idea?" I deadpanned to the doctor after he gave me the results of the scan.

"You did what?" he replied incredulously.

Sorry, but I read nothing in the cancer manuals that prohibited bull riding.

Apparently, playing cowgirl on a bucking bull is frowned upon by doctors when your spine is filled with cancer, because it puts you at a pretty high risk for fractures or paralysis or something. Also note that convincing your doctor it wasn't that big of a deal, because you fell off the bull in a "slow-motion and graceful kind of way to

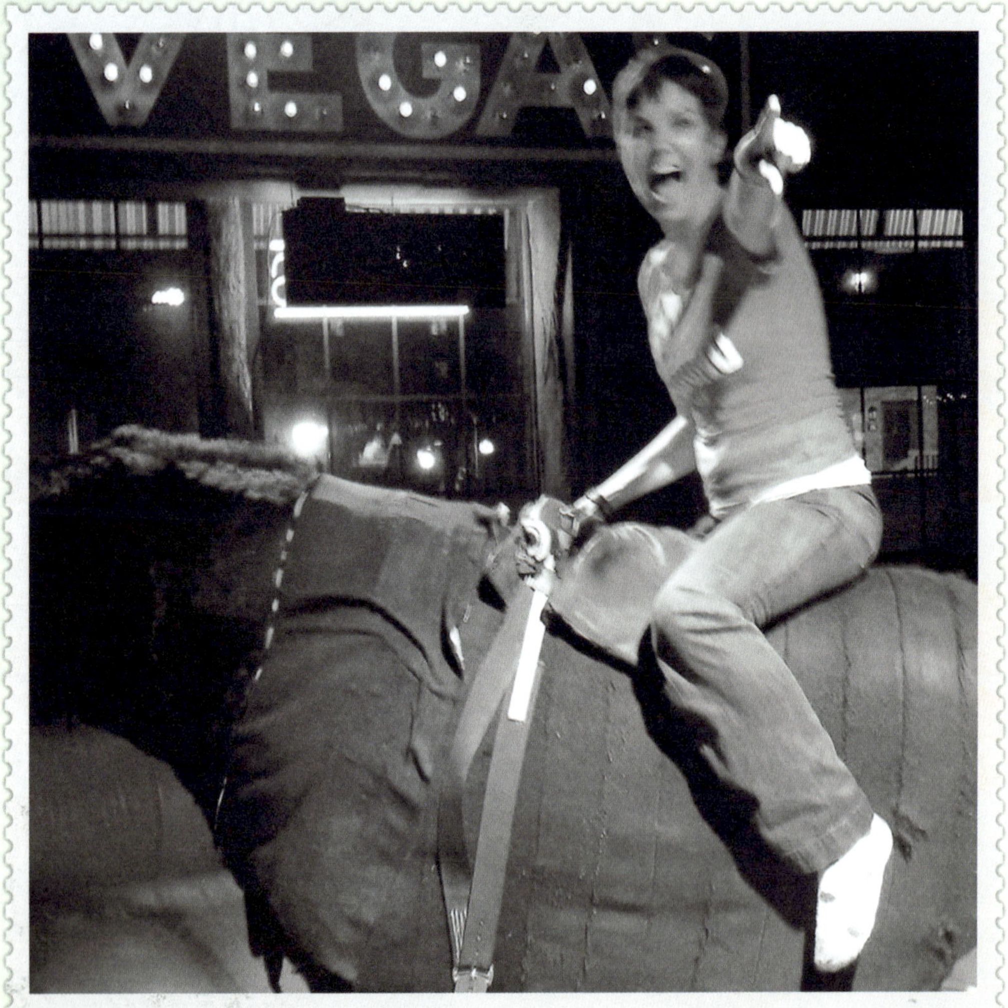
VEGA

raucous applause," will not work.

But instead of saying to myself "Thank goodness I didn't end up paralyzed!" I said "Thank goodness I rode the bull when I had the chance!" Sometimes ignorance really is bliss. If I had had the scan done before my party and knew I was at a high risk for paralysis with cancer in my spine, I (probably) wouldn't have ridden Red Rock. Yes, there are things you shouldn't do in certain situations for the sake of your health, but you also can't live your life in bubble wrap and worry about every possible thing that could go wrong. Do what you can do when you can do it.

About a month after I was diagnosed as terminal, I retired at the ripe old age of thirty-four as a research specialist at the University of Wisconsin School of Medicine and Public Health. In my job, I created databases and data entry processes and developed feedback loops and systems for programs to submit their data and ... I'll stop torturing you there. Let's just call it data management. I loved it! I was charged with finding ways to present data as a story, which satisfied both the organizational and creative realms of my brain. But when multiple doctors stamp an expiration date on your life, you wake up to the reality that there are things you love a whole lot more outside the drab walls of a cubicle farm. (By the way, I was recently enlightened by anonymous sources that my old cube was razed and replaced with a state-of-the-art printer station. FYI to my former coworkers: when I'm gone, I fully intend to haunt that printer.)

Most of my time in retirement has been spent with people no less than seventy years old, which is why I always say old people are my people. If I stop somewhere to get coffee in the morning after dropping Bri off at school, there are the old people having breakfast. If I go to the oncologist's office for an appointment, I'm surrounded by old people in the waiting room. When I hear old people complaining about something, it's usually their aches, pains, Social Security benefits—complaints that mirror my issues. But I've learned we retirees, and all people for that matter, have very little to grumble about if we wisely use the limited time we have in this world to truly live.

I've resided just outside of Madison for nearly two decades and worked in the city for six years, yet I realized when I retired that I'd never taken time to go inside the Wisconsin State Capitol, a spectacular work of art from the outside. Think about the places or sites near your home that you've never stopped to appreciate; some you may pass every day on your way to work or when driving your kids to their tenth extracurricular activity of the afternoon. How would your perspective change toward those things if you knew for certain you were going to be dead soon? To experience is to live. As Ferris Bueller profoundly stated, "Life moves pretty fast. If you don't stop and look around once in a while, you could miss it."

I took that advice and finally visited the Capitol one day, spending three full hours exploring every crevice inside the edifice. One of the highlights is the rotunda. While most people cock their heads ninety degrees and strain their necks to get a glimpse of the dazzling dome two hundred and fifty feet above, I headed straight for the center of the room, laid down flat on the cold marble floor, took several deep breaths, and soaked in the beauty. I heard a few people walk past me and mumble about what I was doing, probably even wondering if I was insane or on drugs. Ironically, it was one of the rare times when I wasn't on any prescribed medication that could have affected my behavior. How cool would it have been if, instead of questioning what I was doing, those people would have followed my childlike curiosity and joined me on the floor? I was high purely on my surroundings. It was such a simple moment, yet so spectacular.

It took me sixteen long years to stop ignoring that building and to discover and appreciate what it had to offer. There's no excuse for that. Nothing so beautiful and accessible should ever take anybody that long to experience. Unfortunately, it took the cancer that's killing me to make me realize it.

Chapter 2

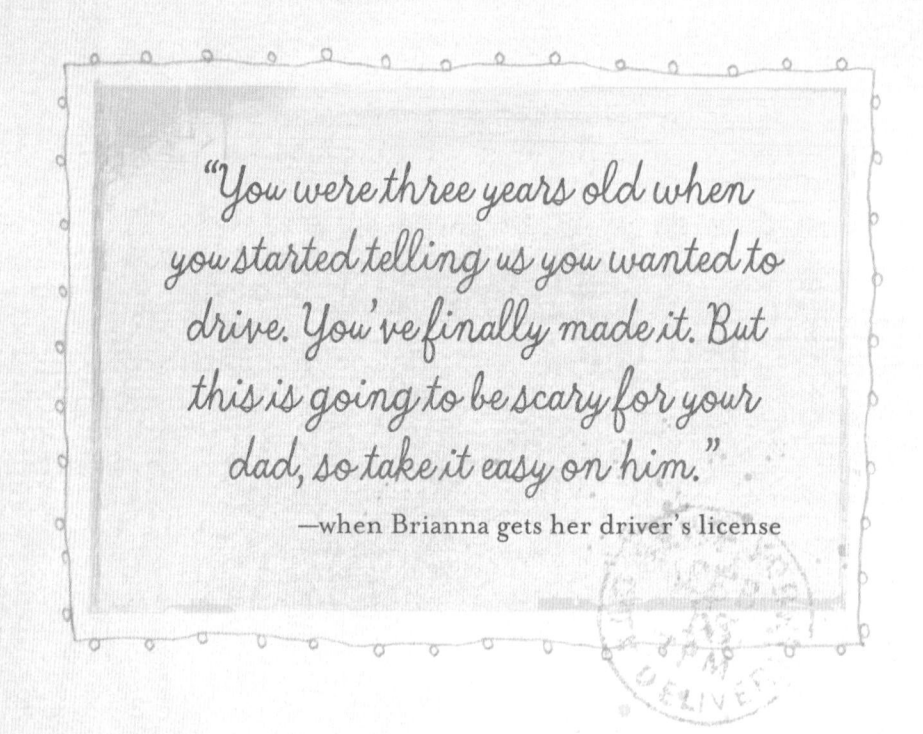

"You were three years old when you started telling us you wanted to drive. You've finally made it. But this is going to be scary for your dad, so take it easy on him."

—when Brianna gets her driver's license

Leaving Love in Good Hands
When Brianna Gets Her Driver's License

Before Brianna was born, Jeff had never once held a baby, and he never even knew what to say to toddlers or older kids. He'd have interacted better with aliens. So when I told him I was pregnant, he freaked out. I mean, freaked out! It took him a few days to digest the news and to talk about it with me. And then when we found out it was going to be a girl . . .

"We're going to have to put a lock on the basement door. There's a wet bar down there," he said with grave concern. "And she's not watching movies down there with boys. No way."

"Wait . . . what?" I replied quizzically. "You do realize she's still a fetus, right?"

But what a difference holding your child for the first time can make. Jeff was a natural at "daddyhood," and to be able to witness the relationship that has developed between him and Bri over the last four-plus years has really been something special for me.

He teaches her all about football. They hang our Wisconsin Badgers flag outside the house every Saturday before UW football games. They go grocery shopping together. Before the cancer came, I did most things with Bri that needed to be done, like giving her baths and getting her ready for bed. But after my mastectomy, Jeff had to go beyond football chalk talk with her. He went from "filling in" when needed to becoming the main caregiver. He has an amazing gut instinct of what a good dad is. At one time I would have thought that I'd have to author a step-by-step instruction guide for him on how to raise Bri when I'm gone, but I don't. He could write the book if he wanted to.

The first time he drove her to preschool, he handed the teacher a rubber band to put Bri's hair into a ponytail.

"Here," he said, exasperated. "I'm clueless on this one."

But now he's mastered even the smallest intricacies. Not only can he put her hair in a ponytail, but he's also learned how to braid it and is proud to do it. I've had a lot of friends with stage IV cancer who didn't have the same comfort level in their partners that I do in mine. I know how very fortunate I am to know Bri will always be in good hands.

That's not to say Jeff won't have challenges, especially when Bri hits her teen years. I know he'll worry to death when she gets her driver's license. Even today, for whatever reason, Bri always seems to nominate Jeff to answer the uncomfortable questions, like "How are babies made?" It's entertaining for me to watch as he stammers and stutters and struggles to spit out something coherent that a four-year-old can understand before I come to his rescue. So what will happen when I'm gone? I don't see her complex questions or his disjointed responses changing when she hits puberty. That's why I've made some audio recordings for her, such as when it's time to have "the talk" or when she has her first menstrual period. All she'll have to do is push a button to hear her mom speaking directly to her about those issues. That may seem like a quirky parenting method, but I believe there are some things for which a girl needs her mom. If, by some miracle, Jeff is perfectly fine handling all the difficult girl talks by himself, then more power to him. He and Bri are welcome to bond some more after their talks by making fun of my recordings. I'll be there in spirit, laughing right along with them.

I know there's always the chance Jeff could remarry and that Bri could have a loving stepmom to help with situations that may require a female touch. Jeff and I have had many conversations about that, and I genuinely hope he finds someone who is great for him and who will be a dedicated mom to Bri. Of course, I won't be here to see it, so maybe that's partly why I'm okay with it. But I truly want him to be happy. He knows that.

If there is any worry I have about leaving Jeff, it's the broken heart I know he'll suffer when I'm gone. From the day we first met more than fourteen years ago, I can count on one hand how many times we've been physically apart. We have always been together because it's where we've always wanted to be; we really are best friends. We assumed when we got married that it was the beginning of something magical that would last for decades. It's very distressing for both of us knowing that our life together will be cut short, that we won't be growing old together.

I know this may sound like a wacky perspective, but our relationship has been absolutely perfect, and I feel that in a world where nothing is perfect and the bad always seems to interrupt the good at some point, it makes sense that I'm dying. To expect a relationship between two people to be this wonderful from the start and to last into old age—I think it's just too good to be true.

I hope my perspective is proven wrong after I'm gone and that Jeff and Bri can carry on the very special father-daughter relationship they've had thus far for a lot longer than Jeff and I have had together. With a piece of me always in their hearts and minds, it would be, for me, the next best thing to being here.

Chapter 3

"Your dad and I always found ways to laugh, even on the worst possible days. There are so many things about dealing with cancer that are beyond ridiculous. If I didn't laugh at a lot of it, I would have gone insane. Believe me when I say that even if you don't feel like laughing now, you will do it again one day soon. Live, laugh, love. Don't ever skip that middle one."

—when Brianna is having a rough day

Laughter Is the Best Medicine
When Brianna is Having a Rough Day

I have several friends with stage IV cancer, and sometimes we'll get on a YOLO kick. I know, we're waaay too old to be using that acronym, but I guess you can say that's a reflection of my YOLO attitude. YOLO stands for "You Only Live Once." The Urban Dictionary defines it as "the dumbass's excuse for something stupid that they did." Probably true in many cases. But I would contend that when you have a terminal disease, not only is having a YOLO attitude not stupid (or solely reserved for dumbasses), but it's also a way to laugh in the face of the one thing every one of us will experience but often struggle to find any humor in: death.

I went in one day for one of my "We're sorry, Heather, but you're still dying" doctor appointments. After receiving the usual grim news, which I'd become numb to, I smiled and asked my oncologist what any patient in my position would ask:

"Can I get more tattoos?"

Here was this nice man trying to find a sensitive way to tell me I was a step closer to being turned into ash and dumped into an urn, and I'm thinking a nice flowing patch of pink flowers over my right shoulder would look pretty awesome. He's thinking Poor Heather. I'm thinking YOLO!

After I convinced him more tattoos were a good idea, I thought, Why get a tattoo on my shoulder? Why not plant one right on my face? Or on my shiny bald head? It's not like I have to grow old with it or worry about a job interview. I didn't take it that far, only because I didn't want to terrify Bri. But that's the freedom cancer has given me—to laugh and find a silver lining in every situation. When a report came out last year that bacon causes cancer, my first thought was, Yes! I can eat as much bacon as I want! After one of my numerous chemo treatments, Jeff joked that I'd have an advantage over everyone else during a zombie apocalypse. He was confident that with all the chemicals that have been pumped into my body—I think I'm only three letters shy of completing the cancer medication alphabet (A

= Adriamycin, B = Barium Sulphate Suspension, C = Carboplatin . . .)—I'd likely survive a nuclear Armageddon.

Actress Audrey Hepburn once said, "I love people who make me laugh. I honestly think it's the thing I like most, to laugh. It cures a multitude of ills. It's probably the most important thing in a person."

Laughter won't cure my cancer, but it certainly makes it a heck of a lot easier to face each day.

Just prior to my mastectomy, I met with a plastic surgeon. Like all of my doctors and nurses since day one, he treated me like a queen. He was a little guy who barely came up to my shoulders. He had a shaved head with big blue eyes and an accent I couldn't identify but loved to listen to. Oftentimes, when we parted ways, he'd put the palm of his hand to my cheek and say, "Godspeed, Heather. Godspeed."

During our first visit with him, he was explaining to Jeff and me what I was about to go through. He shared a touching story of his wife having faced the same thing—a double mastectomy followed by breast implants. He said there was absolutely no way to prepare myself emotionally for what I would see and feel when I woke up from the mastectomy surgery. The emotions, he said, are different for everyone. It's a very personal surgery, unlike any other.

He was very patient and kindhearted when he spoke. He listened attentively and answered every one of my questions and concerns. It was a passionate conversation because the subject matter was so intense, yet he was so graceful and sensitive through it all. I had tears in my eyes as we talked. Jeff firmly held my hand, comforting me every second. It was one of many deeply emotional moments I would experience throughout this ride. And then . . .

The doctor tossed the fake boob.

Leaning forward, with his elbows on his knees and the fake boob in one hand, the doctor softly lobbed it in the air to his other hand as he continued to talk to us in a serious tone. Then he lofted it back to the original hand. And then back again. Like it was a juggling ball. Give him two more fake boobs and some clown makeup and he'd have been a circus act. I was crying from this heavy conversation we'd been having. Jeff was trying to hold back tears. The doctor was softly speaking about the traumatic experience I was about to encounter, never losing eye contact with us. But now, suddenly, all I could think was, Oh my God! Stop throwing the boob!

He continued to toss it and squish it with each catch, like a stress ball. I was still crying, but now most of my tears were out of sheer hilarity. I know he wasn't doing it intentionally, but it would have been fine if he was. It certainly lightened the mood. I know I left his office feeling better than I would have if he hadn't done it. It was one of the first of hundreds of examples since my diagnosis of how during even the most agonizing and serious moments, there is still so much you can laugh about.

In the cancer medication alphabet, I used to have "L = Lorazepam" for the antinausea medication I've taken after chemo, but I've changed it to "L = Laughter." There really is no better medicine.

Chapter 4

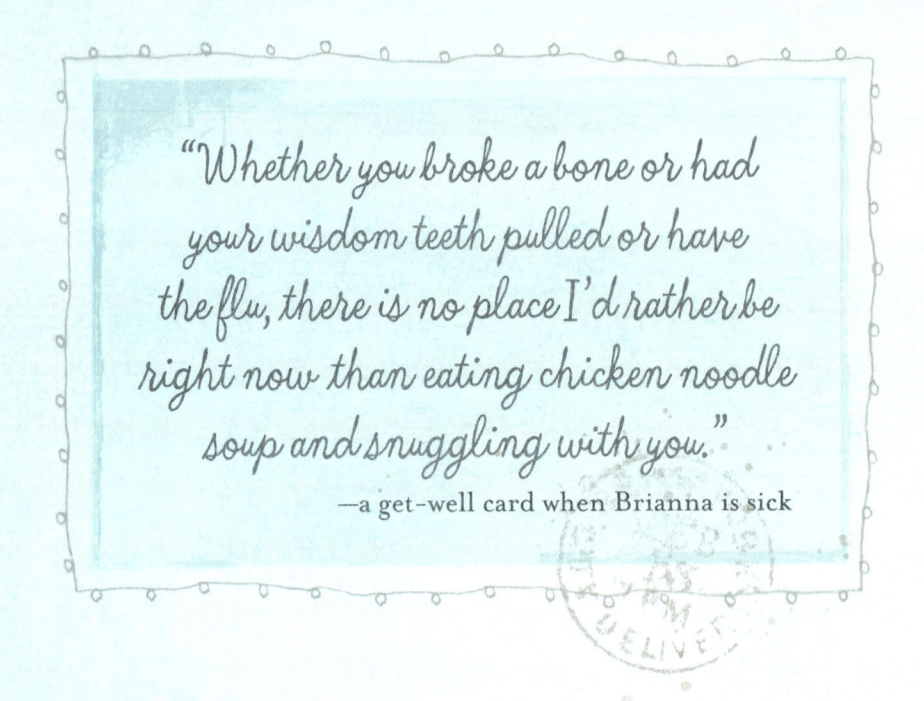

> "Whether you broke a bone or had your wisdom teeth pulled or have the flu, there is no place I'd rather be right now than eating chicken noodle soup and snuggling with you."
>
> —a get-well card when Brianna is sick

Accepting Help
A Get-Well Card When Brianna Is Sick

One of the most difficult things for me to accept after my diagnosis was outside help. I'm organized. I'm efficient. I like to be in control. I want to do everything for myself. But sometimes when you're sick or need help of any sort, you have to slow down, swallow your pride, and ask others to take care of you. Even admitting that my family needed a meal train—when neighbors and friends rotated making us dinner each night so that Bri didn't morph into a chicken nugget—was a tough one for me to accept. But I knew we needed the help, and just as important, I realized others wanted to help. It made them feel good to know they were able to do something for us. Since forming a snuggle train—when everyone fills a shift snuggling on the couch with me—may have raised some eyebrows within the community (though not entirely a bad idea, I must say), some homemade chicken noodle soup certainly went a long way toward reducing our stress.

I learned to truly let go and accept all the help and love people wanted to give me when, weeks prior to officially finding out I was terminal, I was told the cancer had spread to my liver. It was one of my most terrifying days throughout this whole ordeal, and Jeff wasn't there with me. He had planned to go to the appointment, but I didn't feel he needed to. It was supposed to be a routine visit. In fact, I had planned to head straight to work from there. But instead, the liver bomb was dropped. After receiving the horrific news, I was led to a cold, sterile room to begin receiving immediate treatment. While chemo was being pumped into my bloodstream, I made tearful calls to Jeff and others about the latest diagnosis. But through the trauma, I was never physically or emotionally alone.

To say I've received amazing professional support since the day I was diagnosed doesn't do justice to the incredible men and women who have been there for me, from the receptionists to the phlebotomists to the nurses to the doctors. Wisconsinites have ginormous hearts and know how to comfort and take care of people. On that dreadful day, the staff took turns sitting with me, hugging me, crying with me, and sharing stories that gave me some hope, even though we all knew there probably wasn't much hope to be had. They have served as my shrinks outside of my actual shrink's office, and they've all genuinely become my close friends, making me laugh and keeping my mind focused on non-cancer stuff. There is nothing fun about having cancer, but they've certainly made this ride as smooth as it could possibly be.

I can't imagine doing the jobs they do. To develop friendships with people who you know are going to die, to see people "cured" only to have them return with recurrence, to see horrible things happen to good people on a daily basis . . . I used to think there was a limit to the amount of crap the universe could pile on a person. Ha! So not true in the case of these remarkable angels. But they also play a major role in helping people get better. They have a hand in and are witnesses to miracles, maybe as often as they witness heartbreak. It has to be an incredible feeling to be able to give someone a second or even third chance at life, so maybe there is some emotional balance for them. Though they couldn't cure me, their "snuggles" during my darkest times have meant the world to me.

Much to the surprise of many, even though my end is near, I can still dish out snuggles as well as or better than I can receive them. A lot of people are afraid to ask me for help or advice because they know the magnitude of their problems is not likely at the level of mine. But given my situation and unique perspective of life, I'm in a very good position to help people view their difficulties in a different light. Yeah, I may have problems on a bigger scale, but you could still be having the worst day of your existence. I love you, I care about you, and I want the chance to be there for you, too.

One day last summer, I received a call from my doctor. He was concerned about some data he'd just reviewed on my condition and wanted me to come in for an immediate brain scan (sounds frightening, but this has become pretty routine for me). Jeff was at work, so my girlfriend Kate drove me to the hospital. After the scan, I suggested to Kate that we not waste the rest of this beautiful day waiting for the results in a depressing waiting room and worrying about possible bad news that might not even surface.

Kate had been going through a difficult couple of days because her grandmother had just passed away, so we went out and had a multiple glass of wine kind of lunch on a gorgeous patio to talk and relax a bit. It was the type of lunch where nothing gets solved, but your face hurts from laughing so hard. I then suggested we head over to nearby Monona Terrace on the shores of Lake Monona. After admiring the lake for a while, we plopped down on the grass for some extraordinary cloud watching. According to Kate, I really suck at cloud watching. I couldn't pick out any shapes on my own or recognize anything she saw—the brain scan must have siphoned off my creativity. But sucking at cloud watching is still far more glorious than sitting in a waiting room reading magazines about ways to improve my long-term health. Then we indulged in high-fat ice cream and sat in giant terrace chairs. We talked and laughed and lived in the moment. Good wine, blue water, green grass, fluffy clouds, and creamy ice cream on a warm, breezy summer afternoon . . . It couldn't have been better.

I was so glad I could be there for Kate when she needed me. Having witnessed the scary norms of my reality and how things can change drastically without warning, like being summoned for a spontaneous brain scan, she was much more centered after our impromptu lunch adventure than she had been when she woke up that morning. She told me I should turn what I did for her into a business: lunch and conversation full of life—changing perspectives with a young, terminal cancer mom. It's not a bad concept, but I think I'll stick to using my free time to snuggle on the couch with Bri and Jeff until I can't do it anymore.

Chapter 5

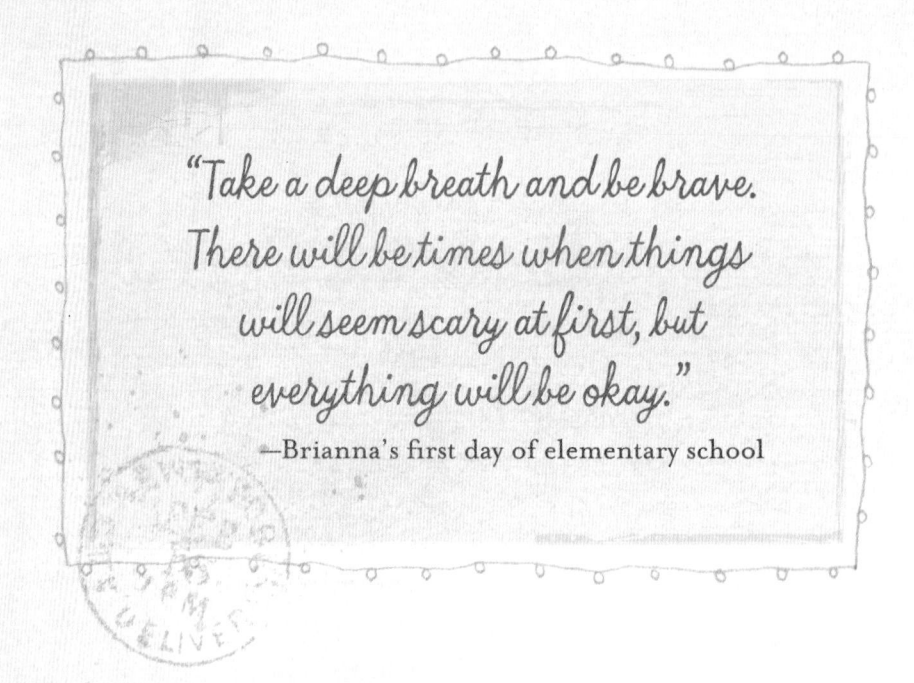

> "Take a deep breath and be brave. There will be times when things will seem scary at first, but everything will be okay."
>
> —Brianna's first day of elementary school

Everything Will Be Okay
Brianna's First Day of Elementary School

I used to know very little about chemotherapy. To me, chemo was chemo. It was a drug injected into your body or taken orally that would kill cancer or at least slow its growth. I had heard horror stories about how it made people sick, but that was a common side effect of the drug that patients had to tolerate. And that was it. I really didn't think there was anything more to know.

Then I got cancer.

I learned the way chemo works is by killing all rapidly dividing cells. It is literally killing you and the cancer with the goal of killing the cancer before it kills you. In other words, it's taking out the good guys with the bad guys, hoping that more good guys are standing when the dust settles. Seriously, it's a little strategy and a lot of luck.

Some of the fastest-growing cells in our bodies are hair follicles, which is why chemo patients lose their hair. But the worst part isn't losing the locks on top of your head; it's losing the nose hair. Do you know how annoying it is to have constant snot dripping, with nothing to catch it or at least slow it down? You don't appreciate the value of nose hair until you don't have any. And having no eyelashes or eyebrows is really uncomfortable because everything gets into your eyes. Fortunately, the eye hair is usually the last to go and the first to come back, maybe a few weeks total. Just don't get all cocky like I did if you ever have to take chemo. I thought I'd be the special one to not lose any of my hair. A lot of people think that going in. But chemo does not discriminate.

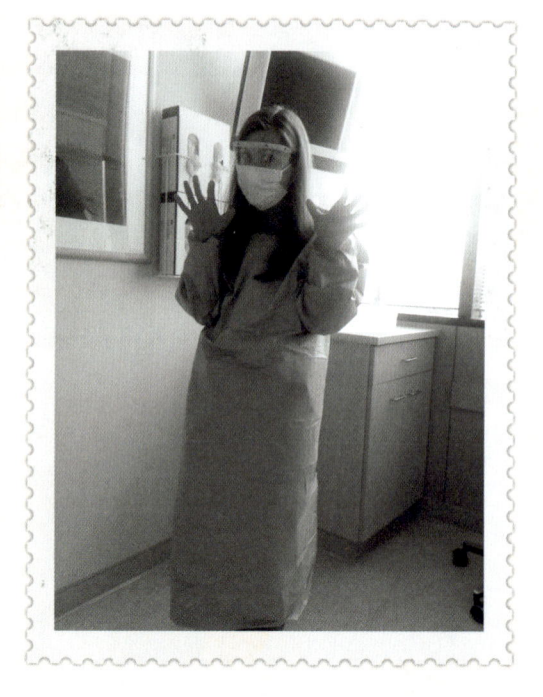

Unbeknownst to me until I started taking it, chemotherapy is not just a single drug. There's Adriamycin, Carboplatin, Taxol, Eribulin, and Xeloda, to name some. I've taken ten different chemo drugs. Side effects include, among many others, nausea, fatigue, loss of hair, loss of taste, and your nails turning gray—assuming they don't fall off first. If you've ever heard people who have received chemotherapy call it "poison" or refer to it as "toxic waste" swimming through their bodies, they aren't exaggerating. Each time a nurse is about to administer it to me, she has to wear a mask, plastic eye shield, full-body apron, and gloves—as if she's entering a biohazard area.

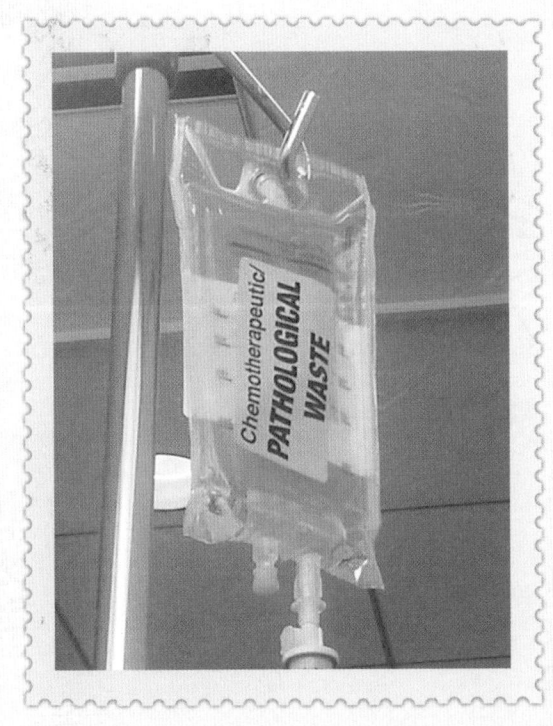

That's because she is.

One bag of my chemo had a big red "Biohazard" sticker on it. Another bag was labeled with a yellow sticker that said "Pathological waste." And yet another, a green sticker, said "Do not dispose down sink or sewer. Place in hazardous waste bin." Because if you pour it down a steel pipe, that would be dangerous. But shooting it directly into my jugular is fine. Adriamycin, commonly called "Red Devil" in the cancer world, was terrifying to me when I took it. It's a red liquid, the original chemo drug from way back when. I've had four doses, and I can't have any more because it's so toxic that it will kill me. The nurses had to be super careful not to get it on their hands when they administered it to me because they said it could burn through their skin. But, again, it's perfectly fine to infuse into my bloodstream.

Chemo is only the beginning, though, of all the fun concoctions you get to ingest when you have cancer. There are steroids, dyes for lymph node mapping, anti-nausea meds, hormone therapy to prevent recurrence (Ha! That worked well!), various antibiotics, hydration fluids, contrast agents for brain MRIs, sedations, medication for chemo fatigue, tasty beverages for CT scans, and wine (that's self-administered at home—it fixes everything).

Each time a chemo drug stops working, I have to go to oncology to get educated about the next one they are going to poison me with. One time, the education consisted of a pamphlet titled "All the Many Horrible Ways a New Chemo Drug Would Totally Suck." At least that's how I read it. Part of taking the new drug required me to also take dexamethasone. Sometimes called "oncology candy," dex (as I affectionately call it) is a steroid that can help curb a multitude of issues caused by chemo, including nausea, loss of appetite, and allergic reactions. While dex helps me with some of those things, I abhor it. My body's reaction to dex can be worse than to chemo itself. It leaves a light on in my brain when I want the lights out. After my chemo treatment, when I just want to sleep, that light keeps my brain churning, sometimes at such a rapid rate that I not only can't sleep, but I can't read, write, or focus on anything.

As I sat in a conference room getting the scoop on the new drug from one of my favorite nurses, she eventually dropped the dex bomb on me.

"You're going to have to take it three times a day for four days," she said as compassionately as you can tell a person to pack her bags for a four-day trip through hell. I've had more than my share of bad news, and I've handled most of it relatively well, but finding out the chemo I was taking had quit on me and that dex was returning to my life was more than I could handle at that time. I burst into tears. Bawled my eyes out, in fact. Went through the whole "life is unfair" mantra. But this was truly one of those moments where the people treating me for cancer went above and beyond just doing their jobs.

Knowing how upset I'd be when she told me about having to take dex again, the nurse was prepared. As I was blubbering like a baby, the conference room door suddenly banged open. Dancing—I'm not kidding . . . literally dancing—through the door with a song blaring on her iPod was another nurse. And she was followed by another nurse. And another. And another. It was a train of eight of them. It was so surreal that I initially had no clue what was going on. And then I realized it was nothing more than exactly what it looked like . . . a spontaneous dance party! In the middle of a hospital! I couldn't believe it. For the next five minutes, we just laughed and shook our booties. Though the party was brief, it was long enough that my problems melted away, my tears dried up, and I smiled a ton. As the nurses headed out, with my mind now more focused on the positive, I thought about Jeff and Bri and why I've gone through the hell of chemo treatments. No, I couldn't avoid having to take dex again and the crap that comes with it, but the nurses raised my spirits enough and got me thinking clearly enough that I knew, as terribly as dex treats me, I was going to be okay.

We all have to do things we don't want to do. Sometimes taking a deep breath, removing ourselves from the heavy emotion of the situation, and taking a lighter or different approach to it can make it tolerable and easier to handle. Chemo sucks. Dex sucks. Everything about cancer sucks times a hundred plus some more. But my daughter and husband are as awesome as awesome can be, and swimming through that toxic river is worth it when I know the two loves of my life are waiting for me at the shore on the other side.

Chapter 6

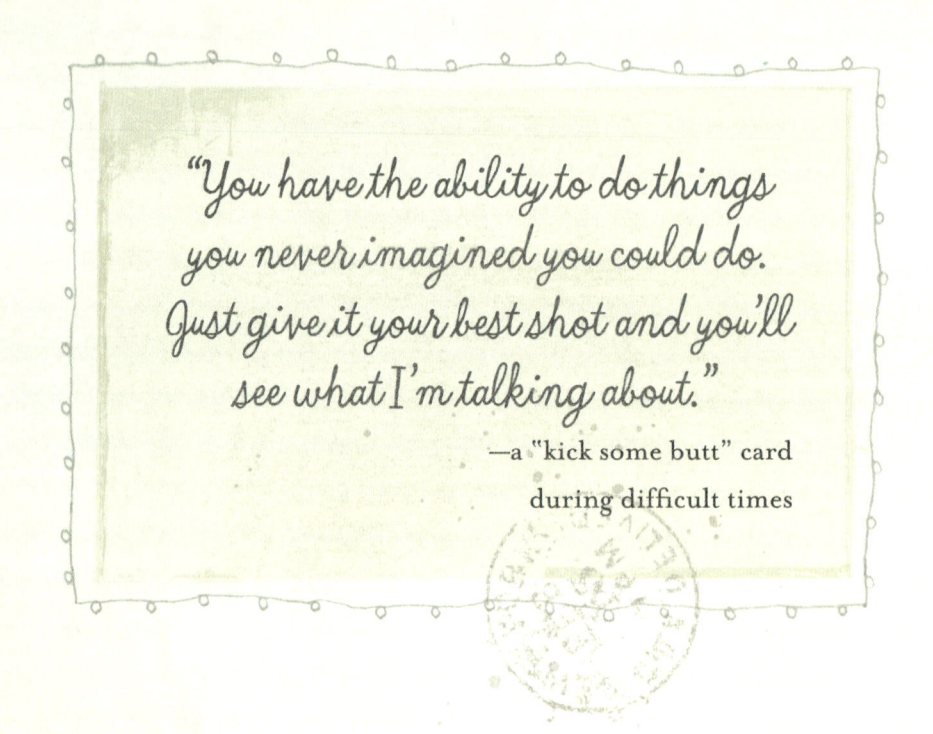

"You have the ability to do things you never imagined you could do. Just give it your best shot and you'll see what I'm talking about."

—a "kick some butt" card during difficult times

Give It Your Best Shot
A "Kick Some Butt" Card during Difficult Times

Long before I ever thought about buying greeting cards for Brianna, I put together some other mementos to help her remember me.

It began with basic Shutterfly and Snapfish picture books loaded with photos of us together. When I first started chemo, before I was certain where this cancer was going to take me, I rearranged my hours at work so I could have every Monday off to spend with Bri. Those days became known as "Mommy Mondays," and they lasted for more than a year, until she started preschool. We filled every Monday with dance classes, gymnastics, a trip to the zoo, play dates, girl trips to water parks, movies, and salon days. We crammed in a ton of fun and captured a lot of it in photos.

Then I started producing videos. I sat on the couch by myself with microphone in hand, rambling into the camera about who I was and what I loved about Bri and how much I would miss her and yada yada yada. I finally had to shout "Cut!" when even the camera looked bored. I worried about how Bri would hear all kinds of wonderful and fantastic things from other people about her mom (I hope) but wouldn't see that same vibrant woman on camera.

So, just like Kramer retooled his format when his talk show on the old Merv Griffin set fizzled out (season nine, episode six of *Seinfeld*, one of my most favorite shows ever), I refocused and decided to do more of a reality show. With my friend's sister and brother-in-law running camera and directing the production, we recorded Bri and me doing everyday things around the house: playing dolls, watching football, making dinner, reading, or just talking about funny or interesting things that happened during our days together. Nothing super exciting, but real-life videos that show the interaction and love between the two of us.

I still made a few videos talking directly into the camera, but with Jeff at my side. We recorded them in the basement while our friends kept Bri occupied upstairs. We bantered about memories like the day she was born and how Jeff and I met. We were both naturally emotional, which certainly added to the charm of the videos. One challenge we had while making them was determining which Bri we were talking to. This was a serious concern when discussing topics like how we met. Would Bri watch this when she was five, ten, fifteen, twenty, fifty? Do we talk to her like she's a child or an adult? Do we make it a G-rated video, or PG, or PG-13? Since no child really wants to know too much about her parents that could push it to a PG-13 rating or worse, we kept it in the G to PG range. Bri tilted it more to a G-rating when, as Jeff and I were talking about a very touching moment in our lives, she escaped from our friends upstairs and busted into the basement bellowing "Twinkle, Twinkle Little

Star." Thank goodness the camera was rolling.

I soon moved on to voice recordings, all very random ones. I recorded myself reading some of her favorite books, and I sang songs to her, including one I sang when she was a baby called "Good Night to You" that I made up to the tune of "Happy Birthday." I can't sing well—I'm awful, in fact—but I could create spur-of-the-moment lullabies with the best of them when my crying baby wouldn't sleep. Of course, as previously mentioned, I recorded the period talk and the sex talk for later in life. I also did some mini interviews with her. We talked about her first day of preschool and the trip we took to Disney World when she was three. That trip to Disney was paid for with generous contributions through a GoFundMe page and by one particularly close group of friends that was determined to have Bri meet Elsa. We swore we'd never go to Disney before Bri was five because we wanted to make sure she would remember it. With us not knowing if I'd live to see her fifth birthday, we went when we could, and it was absolutely magical. Every princess she met was so real to her. I wouldn't be surprised if, with all the pictures we took and the recordings of her and me talking about the trip, she remembers it forever.

After the recordings, I searched Google for "dead mom" to see what ideas would pop up. Morbid? Yes. Practical? Yes. This was before my greeting card story was published, so I didn't have to worry about finding my face covering result page after result page from top to bottom. What I did find were various craft websites with ideas like making customized jewelry and jewelry boxes and other trinkets that include words related to my relationship with Bri, such as "dance," "laugh," and "love." I also found books designed for a mom to record her legacy, such as where she was born, where she worked, her favorite things, and memories of her life.

Of course, I've earmarked some of my personal possessions for Bri, such as jewelry, a journal I kept when I was pregnant, and piles of notebooks we both scribbled in over the past couple years. Everything I've left for her, from these possessions to the videos to the audio recordings, is in Jeff's care. It's completely his call as to if or when she will see any of it. That also includes the famous greeting cards.

I started by buying roughly forty of them. It's now up to about seventy. I got some for Jeff for future special occasions in his life. I also got a few for friends that Jeff will give out when I die, pretty much thanking them for being such great friends and maybe getting in a final zinger (that's how you get the last word). But the vast majority of the cards are for Bri.

My experience writing messages to her in the cards was like most everything else in life that's difficult to do: the anticipation of doing it was far worse than actually doing it. I didn't buy the cards, come home, and joyfully fill them out. I bought them, came home, stared at them for a long time wondering why I had bought them and how in the world I thought I was going to emotionally get through them, and then I put them away for weeks. I couldn't get myself to write in a single one. Part of it was the finality of each one. How do I wish my daughter a happy birthday when I know I won't be here for it? Part of it too was worrying about how she would react when she got a card. What do I say in a wedding card when I have no idea who she will be two or three or however many decades from now, or if I will even matter to her?

I tried to push myself past that obstacle by shifting my mind-set from fear and doubt to Bri's potential perspective of wonderment and excitement when she receives one of the cards. I envisioned her on her wedding day, sitting alone in her beautiful gown in a quiet room, reflecting on life and the ceremony about to take place. Her father walks in with a big, warm smile. He gives her a giant hug and tells her how proud he is of her and how extremely proud her mother would be. It's a warm, touching moment between father and daughter. Jeff then reaches into the breast of his tux and pulls out my card. It says "Brianna" on it in my handwriting.

He hands it to Bri ... and she explodes at him! Just seeing the card makes her bawl uncontrollably minutes before she's supposed to walk down the aisle. The tears cause her once-perfect makeup to stream down her face and drip onto her dress. She screams at Jeff, "How can you do this to me?" as she slams the unopened card to the floor, stomps on it, breaks a heel, and storms out ...

Stop! Just stop!

That's what I had to keep telling myself throughout this process as my mind wandered to fictional worst-case scenarios. I wrestled with so many emotions as I wrote these cards, especially fear and doubt. Would each card add joy to Bri's life or interrupt it? Would the cards make her happy, sad, angry? With Jeff as the keeper of the cards and knowing he would use his best judgment as to whether he should give her a particular one, I continually convinced myself the potential good far outweighed any potential bad. Imagine receiving a card from the person who loved you more than life itself, years after that person was gone. Could there be a better gift? I knew I needed to do this.

I pulled the huge stack of cards from a drawer and got comfortable on Bri's bed one day when she was at school, and I started writing. My notes weren't long, except for the wedding day one, which required extra paper for me to say how much I hoped it was the most glorious day of her life. I didn't worry about my words sounding poetic or profound. I just spoke from the heart and said what I would say if I were handing them to her myself. Hours went by as I completely immersed myself in the moment. Most of the doubts I had about what I was doing gradually faded with each one. It was some of the best therapy I'd ever put myself through. I felt a sense of freedom and comfort knowing that even though I was dying, I would be able to speak to my daughter long after I was gone. And, more important, Bri would be able to hear her mother's voice.

The only doubt that really stuck with each card was "Who will I be to her when she reads this?" I didn't know how to sign some of them. Would I still be "Mom" to her? If Jeff remarries, will his new wife be "Mom," demoting me to "Heather" or "That Woman Who Gave Birth to Me?" If she has a new mom, would I be overstepping my bounds by signing "Mom" or by giving her a card at all? Thoughts like that prompted several spontaneous sobfests. Understand that the thought of wondering if I'd still be "Mom" or not wasn't a negative thing, just a complicated one. To me, for Bri to have a new mom to take care of her would be the best-case scenario. I would honestly be thrilled if that happens! I want to be demoted! But still being here now, trying to figure out how to refer to myself years into the future when I've been gone for a long while and Bri has a new mom, was what I would call "bittersweet joy." A very complicated bittersweet joy.

But, like all the other wild emotions I've experienced through this disease, I just sat with them. I held the card in my lap and the pen in my hand, cried it out until the emotions passed, and then started writing again.

As difficult as each card was to write, the experience was absolutely worth it.

I hope she enjoys the videos and audio recordings and items I made or left for her, but I can't imagine anything will have a stronger impact than a handwritten personal message from me on her special day or in a moment when she could use her mother's love. It won't be a hug or a kiss or a face-to-face talk, but it's the best I can do. And if she doesn't want a particular card, or any of them, that's perfectly fine. They are there for her if she wants or needs them. Just knowing they exist may be therapeutic enough for her.

By the way, I did sign the cards "Mom." I signed a few of them "Heather Mom," which Bri facetiously calls me sometimes. And you know what? In the end, I was one hundred percent content with that. I have no idea who I will be to her years from now, but I concluded that what I think or what worries me is irrelevant. If Bri wants the cards, it will probably be because she remembers me and the special relationship we had, and signing them with anything other than "Mom" or "Heather Mom" just wouldn't be right to her.

Chapter 7

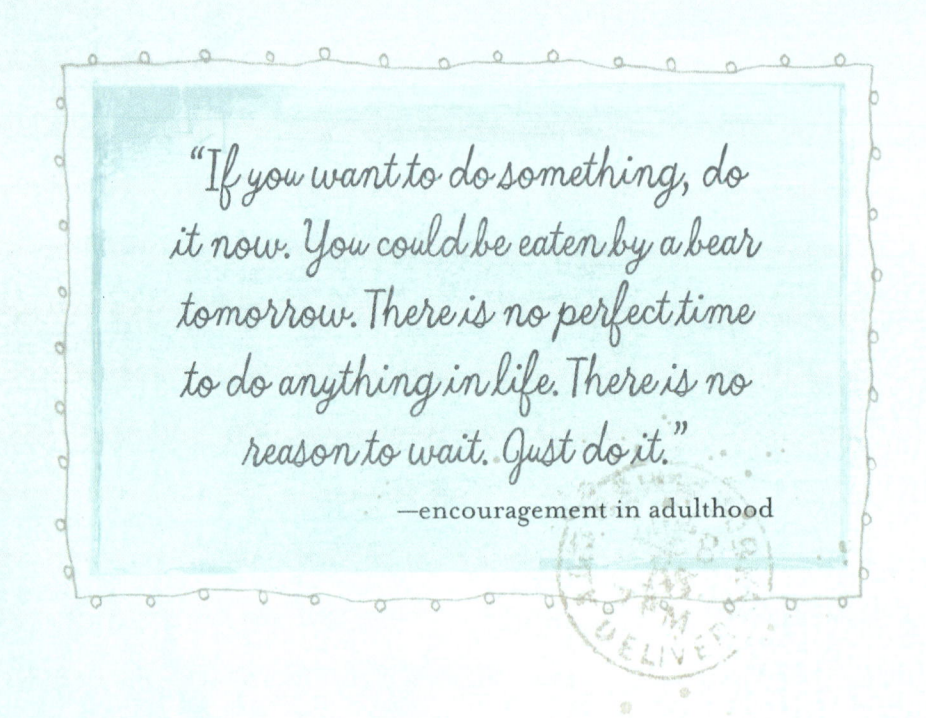

> "If you want to do something, do it now. You could be eaten by a bear tomorrow. There is no perfect time to do anything in life. There is no reason to wait. Just do it."
>
> —encouragement in adulthood

Just Do It

Encouragement in Adulthood

There is no "right" time to do what you want to do. Yes, we have some control over our lives, but I'm living (and dying) proof that much of our fate is beyond our control. If you continue to postpone something you want to do because the timing doesn't seem perfect, there's a pretty good chance you'll never do it.

Last summer, the Do It For The Love Foundation, which gives free concert tickets to wounded veterans and people with life-threatening illnesses, kindly offered Jeff and me tickets to see Mötley Crüe in Milwaukee. We love Mötley Crüe. Let me rephrase that: we love Mötley Crüe! The only "lullaby" Jeff ever sang to Bri when she was a baby was "Home Sweet Home," which she now rocks out to in the living room. We've been to ten of their concerts, and to this day, I really wish we had played one of their songs for the first dance at our wedding (a bit of advice I gave to Bri in another card: do what you want on your wedding day, not what other people want or expect you to do).

The band announced that the world tour they were on would be their farewell tour—to coincide with my farewell tour, no doubt. We knew a couple months in advance that we'd been selected to see the show, but we were uncertain if we'd be able to attend since cancer hates everything I like and does what it can to screw with every aspect of my life.

Three weeks before the concert, I went to the oncology clinic to get injected with a new drug to try to temporarily stave off the cancer's wrath. But just before it was administered, doctors found that my liver enzymes had skyrocketed. To make a long story short, had they given that drug to me with my liver in the condition it was in, it would have killed me within days. Of course, that threw all our plans out the window. The doctors had to nuke me on the spot with the most brutal chemo cocktail I had ever experienced. Manufactured by Satan and his evil elves in hell's underbelly, it knocked me into the hospital where I was hooked to a Dilaudid PCA (Patient Controlled Analgesia) pain pump—one of those pumps where I could push a button to release pain medicine whenever I wanted (why are all humans not equipped with these things?). I pushed the button ninety-three times on just the first day. Yeah, I counted. What else was there to do? I was in so much pain that doctors couldn't determine if it was being caused by a failing liver (bad) or if it was the cancer getting its butt whooped by the chemo (good). Cancer screams when it's dying, so when it's being killed by chemo, its screams are the pain I feel. Of course, if my liver were dying, it too would scream.

The next weekend they gave me only one ingredient of that chemo cocktail (not quite as awful, but still awful), and then I got to take the following weekend off. But they said I'd have to come back for one more treatment the following Thursday—the day before the concert. During that off weekend, we met with hospice under the assumption that if my liver were failing, I would go downhill quickly. That's how grim my outlook was. Seeing my favorite band was no longer a priority. Staying alive was. I called the woman at the foundation to let her know what was happening.

"There's no way we can do it," I told her.

"Don't make that decision yet," she said. "You've got a week before the show, and you don't know yet what will happen or how you'll feel. Let's just wait and see."

A couple days before the show, that same woman sent me an email. She said not only was the foundation going to give us four tickets to the show so that we could take a couple friends, but they also set up a meet-and-greet for me with the band backstage. I was stunned. What an opportunity! But my excitement was tempered. Again, it's cancer. It has its own agenda.

I got my last dose of chemo that Thursday and felt miserable. I told myself there was no way I could go to the show. The next afternoon, on the day of the concert, I had to get some fluids pumped into me for hydration, a normal procedure the day after getting chemo. As I sat there with Jeff, I realized I wasn't feeling so bad.

"You know what?" I said to him. "I'm thinking maybe we should go."

"Go where?" he asked.

"To the concert."

"What? Are you crazy?"

"Maybe, but I'm feeling pretty good," I said with a little pep. "I'd hate to feel good all weekend and not go."

Since doctors are trained to give second opinions, I asked my oncologist what he thought we should do. Mötley Crüe or my living room couch?

"I think you should go," he said matter-of-factly. "There are hospitals in Milwaukee if anything happens."

Well, yeah, duh. I guess when you have cancer, which complicates the heck out of your daily life, you don't always think of things in simple terms like that.

By the time the fluids were in me, I'd convinced Jeff we had to go. We rushed home and packed what we needed, picked up Bri at school, dropped her off at the babysitter's house, and made it to Milwaukee in time for me to meet the band. I felt kinda, sorta, maybe a tiny bit bad that they didn't let Jeff or our friends go backstage with me; I guess you had to be dying to get that privilege. But I managed to get over it pretty quickly. Decked out in my black "I'm not dead yet" T-shirt and shiny purple wig, I played my platinum cancer card with record quickness when it was my turn to meet the guys. It's moments like that for which the card should be used, right?

"Hi," I said with a huge smile as I nervously shook the hand of bassist and band cofounder Nikki Sixx. "I'm Heather, and I'm dying of cancer. Like, really, really soon." There's an icebreaker. I thanked all of them for the wonderful memories they'd given us over the years and told them what a pleasure it was to meet them while we were both on our farewell tours. I didn't expect Nikki, who has led a pretty wild life in the public eye, to be the sensitive one of the bunch.

"Listen to me, Heather," he said with his hands firmly on my shoulders, looking straight into my eyes. "I'm going to do everything I can to make this an incredible show and evening for you. I want you to have the greatest night of your life tonight."

And I did.

Our seats were phenomenal, and it was the best of all the Mötley Crüe shows I'd been to. When it was over, I physically paid for it. I hurt so much from dancing all night that I could barely walk back to the car. I slept the entire next day. But I'd do it all over again if I could. I learned that if you're determined enough to do something and focus on putting one foot in front of the other—literally, in my case—you can do things you never thought you could do. I had a choice: lie in bed all day waiting for the pain and symptoms from my treatment to kick in, or power through and take advantage of an amazing opportunity to meet my favorite band. For the rest of my short remaining life, no matter how bleak and awful my condition gets, I will always be able to smile thinking about that night, and Jeff will have that memory for the rest of his, hopefully much longer, life.

Do what you can when you can do it. Don't live with the regret of not trying something or not doing something you've always wanted to do because you didn't think the time was right. When a bear decides he wants to eat you, he's going to eat you. Bears, like death, don't negotiate.

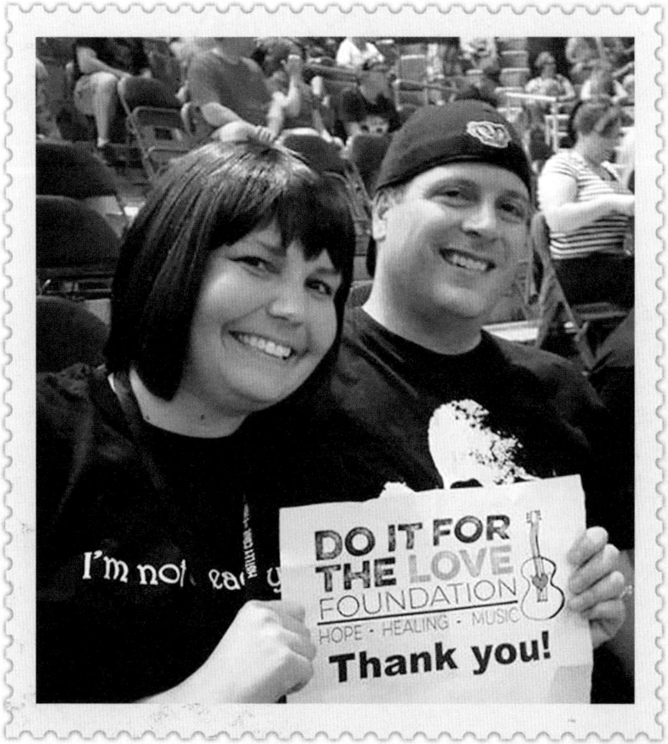
DO IT FOR THE LOVE FOUNDATION
HOPE · HEALING · MUSIC
Thank you!

Chapter 8

> "I used to be afraid to speak in public until I talked about my cancer one day in front of a big crowd of strangers. I realized I not only was pretty good at it, but I enjoyed the heck out of it. Don't let fear stop you from doing anything. And if you fail, so what? Don't regret not trying."
>
> —a "You can do it!" card

Don't Regret Not Trying
A "You Can Do It!" Card

"**In the game of** Survivors vs. Breast Cancer, you're winning! You have stolen the ball from breast cancer, and now it is in YOUR court! We have been cheering for you from the very beginning, and we want to celebrate your success with you."

That message was in an email I received from the local chapter of a national breast cancer organization about a month after I was sucker punched in the liver with the news that my cancer had metastasized, there was no hope to cure it, and I likely had two years at most to live. Talk about adding insult to injury. Here's my own basketball analogy: the cancer in me, a team of Michael Jordan clones in their prime, is beating me by fifty points with a minute left in the game and is still applying a full-court press. I can call a time-out every now and then to slow down the pace, but the outcome has been decided. We're just waiting for the final horn to sound.

As someone whose life has been dictated by breast cancer for nearly three years, and whose death is expected to come soon because of breast cancer, I appreciate any efforts from anyone to combat this disease. But I feel the pink ribbon narrative we see everywhere today, especially each October, has run its course and needs a shift in focus. I think people and organizations that support the pink ribbon story have their hearts in the right place. It's good that they have created a community where breast cancer survivors can find and support one another, and the awareness that has been brought to the disease is unmatched. But we should be well beyond the awareness stage. That effort has become so commercialized, and I feel those of us whose cancer has metastasized—"mets" is what we call it, and "metsters" are what we call ourselves—have been left out of the conversation because we're in stage IV and don't fit that pretty pink narrative.

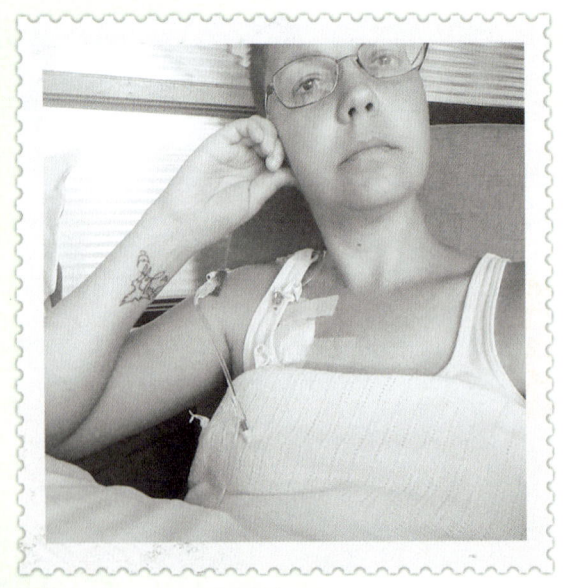

We metsters are dying. One hundred and ten of us in the United States vanish every single day—nearly five an hour. We're not in a "battle." We're not the "happily ever after" story people like to hear. There's no "awareness" that will help us. Call us strong. Call us brave. But we're not survivors, despite the fact that we did exactly what awareness campaigns told us to do. I had no family history of breast cancer. I was just thirty-three when I was diagnosed. The cancer was only in stage II at the time. I had a double mastectomy less than a month after it was discovered, and I followed that with aggressive chemo treatments for more than a year. Then came the death blow. It still makes me cringe to remember Jeff's celebration about a month after the mastectomy, when we were told "Technically cancer-free!" Jeff fist-pumped. We celebrated, cried, texted everyone. We thought that was it! We just had to do chemo for roughly the next year, and we could put cancer behind us! This is what I and countless other women in stage IV still don't understand. I know so many women who have been told the cancer is gone, only to be blindsided later with the grim reality that it has spread and they are actually dying. Where is this awareness? It didn't matter that I discovered the cancer quickly (several years before I was expected to get my first mammogram) or that I did everything I could to treat it. Only one thing mattered: my pathology.

Consider this comment by Dr. Eric P. Winer, director of the breast oncology center at the Dana-Farber Cancer Institute in Boston, in a *New York Times* article: "All too often, when people think about breast cancer, they think about it as a problem, it's solved, and you lead a long and normal life; it's a blip on the curve. While that's true for many people, each year approximately 40,000 people die of breast cancer—and they all die of metastatic disease. You can see why patients with metastatic disease may feel invisible within the advocacy community."

There's a pink cap on my medications that says "Early Detection Saves Lives." Well, yeah, it might save your life. But it might not. Yes, get your mammogram when you should, maybe even sooner. But you need to know that may not be enough. That's why finding a cure needs to be priority number one. Then, and only then, will this disease truly be beaten.

The commercialization of breast cancer is obvious, and it's so overwhelming that it never lets those of us with cancer forget we have it, even for just a day. I can't watch a football game in October without seeing pink shoes, pink gloves, pink uniforms, pink penalty flags, and fans wearing pink hats and jerseys. In stores and online I've found pink ribbon mushrooms, pink ribbon yogurt-covered pretzels, pink ribbon watermelon, pink ribbon eggs, pink ribbon pepper spray, and pink ribbon stun guns. Yes, pink ribbon stun guns. While millions of volts of electricity are charging through your body, remember: Early Detection Saves Lives.

So, if I were in charge, what would I do differently?

First, in terms of awareness, I would make an effort to bring awareness to every cancer. Breast cancer gets most of the focus. Why limit awareness to only one type? How much do we know about other cancers? Thousands of women die each year of ovarian cancer. What do you know about detecting and treating ovarian cancer? I know I've personally never been educated about it. If awareness is going to be created for cancer in one part of the body, let's do it for the whole body.

Second, much more money needs to go toward finding a cure. Creating awareness is good. Research to find a cure is far better. There isn't anything more I can say about that.

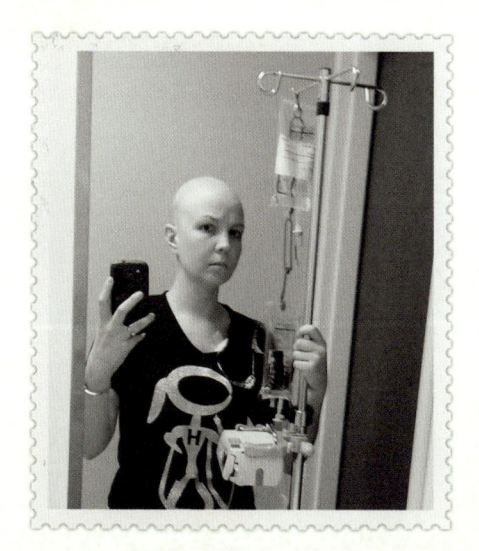

Third, include everyone with cancer, from stages I to IV and with all types of cancer, in the discussions. Men can get breast cancer too, but not many people are aware of that fact. Peter Criss, original drummer with the rock band KISS, is one of the more well-known men who have had it in recent years. For metsters, especially those who are fairly young, like me, there are very few resources and little advice on how to live with stage IV. So many of us feel isolated. Not only have we been repeatedly asked in support groups to "sugarcoat" our conditions so we don't upset others in the group who still have a chance to survive, but would you believe some of us metsters have been asked to leave support groups? Really. They see us as the grim reapers in the room. Believe me, the last thing I want to do is scare anybody, but I can't change my reality. There need to be more resources readily available for young metsters because, like it or not, we're not dead yet. We still have lives to live. I've had to practically stalk people on social media to find fellow metsters, and I can't state strongly enough the importance of the bond we've created and how much these women have changed my life for the better. I am eternally grateful for each of them. We help one another with how to live the rest of our short lives—but only after we find each other, which isn't easy.

I feel so strongly about these issues that they have inspired me to overcome one of my biggest fears: public speaking. It used to make my stomach turn thinking about having to give a talk in front of others. Even if I just had to speak at a small work meeting with people I knew, I would try to find excuses not to go. I'm not proud of this, but when I was pregnant with Bri, I continually postponed a fifteen-minute presentation I was supposed to give until I knew there was no way I could do it prior to maternity leave. That's how terrified I was of public speaking. However, since I was diagnosed with mets, I've thrown myself in front of crowds as large as a thousand people, and usually with nothing prepared in advance. No rehearsal. No note cards. I simply speak from the heart. At first I did it with tremendous reluctance. Now I do it with immense passion and excitement. I realized that I could not keep quiet and let opportunities like that slip by. Based on the applause and comments

I've received, I guess I'm pretty good at it, so I've taken my newfound "talent" to social media, openly sharing my story and giving a voice to all metsters. It may not be an NFL field on a Sunday afternoon in front of seventy thousand people and a national television audience, but every worthy cause has to start somewhere.

I feel, in a sense, that I'm bucking the pink ribbon trend—but I'm not anti-pink ribbon, and I don't want to minimize what good the pink ribbon awareness campaign has done, and is still doing, for other women. I just want people to understand that it does not represent those of us in stage IV, and not everyone currently in the early stages will avoid stage IV just because they are following certain "awareness" protocols. I feel like we're at a point when we need to go beyond the pink ribbon mushrooms and stun guns and put more time and resources into research to find a cure for all cancer. I've lost three amazing friends to metastatic breast cancer in the last six months. That translates to six small children without mothers today. Resources are lacking for those facing terminal diagnoses. I won't have a voice for very long, but I feel compelled to speak up with the hope that others will be encouraged to take up this cause with me now—and without me when I'm gone.

Those of us with mets exist. Our stories aren't pretty, but we matter. Awareness can help save lives. Research and a cure will save lives. Not mine, but maybe someone else's. Maybe even Bri's.

Chapter 9

"I know you—you're awesome! Don't let anyone tell you otherwise. Being a teenager isn't easy. It may feel like the world is falling apart sometimes, but you'll get through it. And if you ever need a girl to talk to, I have lots of girlfriends who will listen."

—Brianna's thirteenth birthday

Comfort In, Dump Out
Brianna's Thirteenth Birthday

When my oncologist officially classified me as terminal, Jeff and I wordlessly shed a few tears in the clinic (though I do believe I may have muttered a few choice words not suitable for print) before heading to the car. We sat in the parking lot dumbfounded and silent, not sure what to do. Our eyes were fixated out the windshield and into the distance, in disbelief that we were having this experience again, sixteen months after my initial diagnosis of breast cancer and more than a year of treatment that was supposed to make me all better. I occasionally looked over at Jeff and shrugged. How could we even try to make sense of something so unfair? But we knew we had to come up with a plan . . . and what better way to do it than over some wings and beer? We'd been in the oncology clinic for more than five hours. I was hungry and thirsty and dying. While wine is the ultimate treatment for making bad things better, good food coupled with beer is a close second.

What we decided, without question, was that we were going to live normal lives. Sure, it would be a new normal; there was no avoiding that. Actually, it would be a "new new normal." My new normal was when I was first diagnosed, when I had to adapt to life with early stage breast cancer. Now I had to adapt to life with forever cancer. In this new new normal, I would quit my job so I could spend more time with Bri. My days would be filled with countless doctor appointments and oddball symptoms, like agonizing pain in places on my body I didn't previously know existed, seeing rainbow sparkles circling around my head from tumor fevers, and peeing every color in the spectrum from medications. But we wanted to stay in control of as much as possible. We weren't going to cancel plans or tiptoe around my disease or not tell people about it. We felt the healthiest thing to do would be to be ourselves and hope everyone else would follow our lead.

We've received an astounding amount of support from friends and family, so much that we will never be able to repay them. Thriving as well as we have in our new normal and new new normal would not have been possible without them. Whether it's organizing meal trains, sitting with me for hours through chemo and actually making it fun, ensuring that Bri's routine stays as ordinary as possible (making it to dance classes and play dates, even when plans change without warning), doing housework and yard work for us, dragging me to oncology for fluids (when I usually argue that I'm fine), or just being there to talk to, we couldn't ask to be surrounded by more genuinely amazing people. When we broke the news to everyone that the cancer was terminal, it was difficult for them to accept. But I've always been an open book, and I told them this issue was going to be no different. Nothing was out of bounds to talk about. It would only be as awkward as they chose to make it.

A couple weeks after we shared the news, we hosted our annual Badgers football game party. As is often the case with the topic of death, people who came to the party dealt with my diagnosis in their own ways. A few of them kept to themselves a little more than usual because they were still emotional and uncomfortable talking about my situation. Some who did talk to me about it said for as healthy as I looked and acted—referencing the Dirty Girl Mud Run that I had done four days before my diagnosis—they couldn't believe I was dying. I think two things almost everyone had in common were that they kindly offered help in whatever ways Jeff and I needed, and my forthcoming death was a reality check for them that we are all mortal and could go at any time. Many of them simply didn't know what to say to me, and I honestly was fine with that. It was a party, not a funeral. I knew what they wanted to say to me would be expressed in time at the appropriate moment and in the right environment. "Normal" is all Jeff and I wanted in our lives starting with that party, and our friends did a good job that day of helping us achieve it.

But in the months after the party, the devastating news made it crystal clear how to prioritize friendships in my short time remaining. I certainly wasn't looking to do that, but it often became painfully obvious that some people weren't genuine in their concern for us. They were nosy, fishing for gory details, pestering me constantly for updates so they could gossip and have "dying friend" stories to fill conversations with others instead of trying to help us through tough times. After living with terminal cancer for this long, I'm still surprised at the variety of ways some people are able to make my situation all about themselves.

There was a fantastic article in the *Los Angeles Times* in 2013 by Susan Silk and Barry Goldman about the "Ring Theory" of kvetching (complaining), or "Comfort In, Dump Out." The way it works is to draw a circle. In the center ring goes the name of the person experiencing the trauma (me). A larger circle is drawn around the first one. In that ring goes the name of the person who is next closest to the trauma (Jeff). Rings and names continue to be added. When finished, the result is called a "Kvetching Order." The rules are that the person in the middle can complain about anything to anyone at any time. Everyone else can do the same, but only to those in outer rings. When talking to someone in an inner ring, the goal is to help that person. Comfort in, dump out. And if it seems unfair, as the article states, "Don't worry. You'll get your turn in the center ring. You can count on that."

I found early on that trying to make people feel better about my cancer and diagnosis was too mentally and physically exhausting. It was almost all comfort out, dump in. I was often asked by friends to promise not to die because it would be too upsetting for them (I guess more upsetting than it is for me or my daughter or my husband). I was even told multiple times not to use the medically accurate word "terminal" because it was too negative, to which I replied, "Um . . . but we're all terminal." I had more than I could hold on my plate with trying to work, be a good mom and wife, not die, and just generally function. Other grown-ups were responsible for their own feelings, and I needed to take care of my family first.

Of course, a terminal diagnosis also confirms who your closest and best friends are. Some of my friends who share my dry and morbid sense of humor even grew comfortable enough to joke with me about the fact that I was dying. One day, a girlfriend and I were hiking when several vultures circled overhead.

"What in the world are they looking for?" I said.

"Probably you," she replied.

Had we been standing on the edge of a cliff, I'd have fallen over it laughing. (I've always said that just because I have terminal cancer doesn't mean that's how I'm going to die. Anything can happen at any time.)

The most gratifying piece of support for me through this very difficult time hasn't been what others have done for us to date (though all very much appreciated, of course), but what several of my girlfriends have promised to do for Bri when I'm gone. One friend told me she notices the cute clothes I pick out for Bri and that she would make sure Bri continues to be dressed stylishly. Another friend has offered to teach Bri how to apply makeup when she's old enough. Several have said they will be there for Bri when she needs a woman to talk to, whether it's about boys or school or whatever. One is going to make sure Bri keeps her awesome sense of humor. And they all said they'd make sure at least one of them is at every one of her dance recitals.

A couple weeks after my terminal diagnosis, several of my girlfriends came over to the house and spent time with Bri to show me how serious they were about taking care of her. Bri had met all my friends before, but usually with other kids around. On this day, Bri was the only kid and "just one of the girls" as they showered her with attention. "Mommy, now that I hung out with your friends, they are my friends too, right?" she asked me after they'd left. She still refers to that day a lot, which warms my heart.

I know when I'm gone that Bri is going to be raised by a much larger village than the one that raises her now. My death is not going to be easy for her. We meet regularly now with a child psychiatrist, who will also be on call when I'm gone. I have tapes and DVDs for Bri to listen to and watch. I have cards for every occasion for the rest of her life. But it's going to be those friends who are going to get her through a lot of her struggles. And for a dying mom who will no longer be able to fulfill her obligations and desires as Bri's mother, there is no greater peace for me than knowing that they will be there.

Chapter 10

"Sometimes you need to get a bottle of wine, curl up on the couch, and watch reality TV all day. Do the mental health thing every now and then and take a break from life. Cry and wallow and have a pity party for yourself. Just make sure you crawl back out the next day."

—for a relationship breakup or just a bad day

Take a Break From Life
For a Relationship Breakup or Just a Bad Day

It makes me sad to reminisce over photos of myself from my pre-cancer days, because that life died once the cancer ravaged my body. It's also torturous to think about the future life I might have had, because the cancer, for all intents and purposes, killed that person, too.

I may make whimsical comments about my impending doom (there's another one), but I really do mourn . . . a lot. Every one of the thousands of times that I've been mercilessly knocked down and stomped on by the cancer, I've managed to scrape myself up, only to be blindsided by something else—more tumors, another side effect, a treatment that no longer works—and sent reeling once again into a deep black hole. Cancer chips away at you in the slowest and cruelest way possible until there's nothing left. I wouldn't be human if I wasn't psychologically wounded by the countless blows it has dealt me.

To help me through this incessant hell, I try to apply my psychiatrist's simple, four-word piece of advice to every minute of each day: Live in the moment. Forget the past. Forget the future. They don't matter. Now is what matters. Live. Laugh. Love.

Sometimes after Bri leaves for school in the morning, I'll sit on the couch for several minutes and stare out the window. No TV, no phone, no agenda. I don't think of anything in particular. I just let myself "be." I liken it to the *Seinfeld* episode in which Elaine and her boyfriend, David Puddy, are on an airplane. While Elaine reads a book, Puddy stares straight ahead at the back of the seat in front of him, and he seems perfectly content doing it for the entire flight. That boggles Elaine's mind.

"Want something to read?" she asks Puddy.

"Nah, I'm good," he says, continuing to look straight ahead.

[long pause]

"Are you gonna take a nap or . . . "

"Nah."

[long pause]

"You're just going to sit there, staring at the back of the seat?"

"Yeah."

After another long pause, Elaine explodes and breaks up with him. I'm proud to say that I'm like Puddy, able to simply "be" in the moment without any distractions or the need to be entertained (fortunately, there's enough substance in my relationship with Jeff that he's stayed with me through my what-appear-to-be-mindless stares). I don't know that it's necessarily meditation. I'm just there.

Whatever you want to call it, it works. It makes me feel good. It's calming. It's now.

My shrink (a shrink is an absolute must after a terminal diagnosis, since cancer takes tremendous joy in trying to crush your sanity—because destroying you physically isn't satisfying enough) is the one who has taught me how to live in the moment by practicing "impeccable self-care." Sometimes, exactly what I need to feel better in a particular moment pops right into my brain—a giant mug of coffee, a long walk, a Bloody Mary with breakfast, or a nap. But for the times when I've felt like nothing could ease my pain, I have learned that I wasn't looking in the right places. All I needed to do was put my hand on my heart and let myself feel and hold the pain until it passed. To sit and really feel is an amazing experience, one that ultimately makes me much stronger.

As a youth and into adulthood, I never, ever cried. Not for any deep psychoanalytical reasons that I know of. I just didn't. I crammed any bad feelings down where I felt they belonged, and everything seemed good. So when I started regularly meeting with my shrink and learning how to live in the moment, it took a lot of effort to let myself fall apart. The first couple times I did, I was a blubbering mess and seriously wondered why this was a good thing. How would I ever be able to piece myself back together? But I did, and I still do. Yes, it's scary to relinquish control of your feelings to the unknown, and it can take a while to recover. But I always manage to navigate my way to the light on the other side, because releasing those emotions helps me to see and feel all the joy in my life.

On some days, my emotions are sparked by heartbreak—the thought of dying, the thought of Bri not having a mom, the thought of Jeff becoming a single parent. Other days, I blame the physical pain. Oftentimes, it's both. But no matter what the cause is or how heavy those feelings are, I've learned to just let them happen. Emotions are natural. They don't like being told what to do or where to go. It took me a couple decades to realize that. I don't stuff them down anymore because they don't belong down there. I allow them to emerge, let them pass through me for however long it takes—which may require an extra glass of wine or an extra hour of mindless television on the couch—and I eventually resurface a stronger person once they're gone.

Most of my emotional moments are the result of quick jabs in the gut. One day,

Bri and I were at Toys"R"Us when she climbed into one of those battery-operated Barbie cars and drove it up and down the aisle. I immediately realized that was the closest I would ever get to seeing her drive. It was a moment that smacked me upside the head and ripped my heart out. Who would've expected that in a toy store? I didn't, but I let it happen. I cried right then and there for a few minutes until I felt better. There were a couple curious stares from fellow customers, but nothing more. I've realized most people don't notice when I cry, or they mind their own business. Maybe they're intimidated by the bald woman sobbing over a Barbie car. Whatever the reason, I usually don't get a second glance. Even if I did, I know the value of letting my emotions naturally flow is so huge that I wouldn't care.

Another punch-in-the-gut moment occurred one New Year's Eve. Jeff and I were on the couch watching TV, laughing and in good spirits, as we watched the ball drop in Times Square. But when the cameras cut to loved ones hugging and kissing each other, it triggered a flood of sadness. My heart crumbled. The New Year is all about new beginnings, like engagements and midnight kisses, and the general excitement of starting something fresh. Jeff and I had celebrated it so many times together . . . but would this be our last one? I bawled my eyes out at that thought—an ugly, snot-nosed cry. Then I finished a bottle of champagne and fell asleep exhausted. When I woke up the next morning, I felt awful about ruining our evening. Was this how it was going to be from now on? What if every special occasion I have left is overshadowed by my grief? But Jeff assured me it would be okay and that my spontaneous outbursts wouldn't ruin anything. It might suck for a brief time, but fortunately, I have become very efficient at coming out the other side. If it hits, I let it happen, and then I anchor back into the now. This was true at the Mötley Crüe concert when they started playing "Home Sweet Home." I started sobbing the second I heard the first few notes. Instead of fighting it, I let it happen, then circled back into the now by singing the song off-key at the top of my lungs in Jeff's ear. It turned a brief, sad moment into one of the most special memories I've ever had with Jeff.

I cry in front of Bri often. I've taught her it's okay to be sad and to release your emotions. Sometimes when I'm sitting on the couch with her while she's napping, I'll cry as I watch her sleep. Last fall, I had to miss her best friend's birthday party after promising I'd do everything possible to go. I was in too much pain to walk or even sit. I was upset because I had missed this same friend's party the previous year after a horrible reaction I had to a medication commonly referred to as "bone glue" (if your pharmacy doesn't have it, check aisle six at your local hardware store). Bri still brings it up that I missed that party, and I swore, for that reason, I would do everything possible to go to this one ... but I couldn't. When we were driving home from the store after getting her friend's present, she asked me about the party. Of course, I cried.

"Mommy, why do you have your sad face? Because you want to go to Macy's party?"

"Yes, and I'm sad I can't go. But I'll cry for a little while, and then I'll feel better. I'm happy you get to go, and I can't wait to hear about it."

"Because if you cry, sometimes you aren't sad anymore."

"Well, yes, and sometimes you are, but that's okay too. But don't worry, I'll be so happy that you're having fun. I'll have the biggest smile on my face."

"Mommy, you've had your sad face a lot. Is it because you don't feel well?"

"Yes. And it's frustrating because I don't want to need to rest so much. I want to dance and run and play with you."

"But the doctors are trying to get the cancer out, right? And if they get the cancer out, you'll feel better!"

"Yes, they're trying really, really hard."

"But you can still jump with cancer, right?"

"Yes! And cuddle you. And even if I'm sad or not feeling well, I always love you."

My hope is that by teaching her it's okay to go to a sad place when you feel you need to be sad, she will be able to better deal with her emotions when I'm gone and, ultimately, be a happier person.

Former North Carolina State basketball coach Jim Valvano, who died of cancer in 1993, said in a very famous speech that there are three things we should all do each day: "Number one is laugh. You should laugh every day. Number two is think. You should spend some time in thought. And number three is you should have your emotions moved to tears, could be happiness or joy. But think about it. If you laugh, you think, and you cry, that's a full day. That's a heck of a day. You do that seven days a week, you're going to have something special."

That's exactly how I've lived my life with cancer, and believe me (and Coach Valvano)—it's an amazing way to live. I feel like my life is spread across a wide field of intense emotions. Yes, it can be painful, even brutal at times, but when you emerge on the other side, life is much brighter and much more beautiful than you ever could have imagined.

Chapter 11

> "I know how hard it is when a pet dies, and I'm sorry it happened. Mourn as long as you need, but know that one day you'll go from being sad every time you think about your pet to smiling about how wonderful it was to have it."
>
> —the death of a pet

Mourn as You See Fit

THE DEATH OF A PET

We bought Bri a fish. Goldie was her name. She was a big, wonderful, loving fish who brought an abundance of happiness into our home ... for forty-eight hours. Just two days after Goldie became part of our family, after we'd put Bri to bed that night, Jeff and I found Goldie belly up in her bowl. Despite unsubstantiated rumors of foul play, a thorough investigation determined she died of natural causes.

And Jeff was freaking out about it.

It wasn't so much that Goldie was dead—I was able to console Jeff about that. (Though he really did spend a lot of time on Google that night trying to figure out why she died. My theory of "Dude, it's a five-dollar goldfish; it's what they do" was not taken seriously.) What he was freaking out about was that we had to somehow tell a four-year-old that her brand-new pet, who had become the love of her life the moment Goldie was randomly scooped out of a store aquarium and plopped into a clear plastic bag, was gone. Our dog, Mitzie, whom Jeff and I had had for several years, died when Bri was three, but Goldie's death was a little different. Bri was now a year older, and Goldie had been her pet, chosen by her and kept in her room.

During his panic of how to handle it, Jeff came up with an idea. He would flush Goldie down the toilet, then go out and get a new fish that looked just like Goldie (in other words, he'd go get another random goldfish). He would then slip Goldie II into the bowl and all would be well.

Not a bad plan, especially given the time crunch we were under in finding a solution by morning, but I thwarted it because I didn't want to lie to Bri about Goldie's passing. Maybe even more importantly, I was all comfy and settled in for the evening and didn't want Jeff leaving me to go to Walmart for a fish. When Bri woke up the next morning, after Jeff spent a sleepless night worrying about how to break the news to her, he went into her room to tell her the truth.

"Honey, I've got some sad news," he said. "Goldie got sick, and ... well, she died."

Bri silently stared at him. Jeff waited for the tears.

And he waited.

And he waited.

No reaction. Maybe she wasn't fully awake yet. He waited a little longer, giving her time to process it—and because he didn't know what else to say. Finally, she responded.

"That's okay. Can I get another one?"

He lost a night's sleep for that response.

"Yeah, I guess. Sure," he replied.

"Where is Goldie?" Bri asked.

Jeff was ready for that question and tried to play it cool.

"Well, we took her to the lake and put her in there. That way, she can be with the other fish." Goldie was actually flushed to sea, but that little fib was okay with me. We made it through the death part—no reason to risk upsetting her at that point. Jeff waited again for her reaction.

"Okay, but next time I have a dead fish, can you leave it in the bowl so I can see it?"

"Sure," he said with relief. Crisis averted.

Everyone mourns differently. Some people compartmentalize their feelings. They want to "move on" as swiftly as possible. Others let their emotions flow as they linger in sadness for days, weeks, months, or even years. Those two types of mourners generally don't mesh. The compartmentalizers think you have to appear as resilient as you can all the time because life doesn't stop for anyone. The lingerers think holding your sadness in is bad for your long-term mental and physical health.

And then there are the four-year-olds who just need to watch an episode of Yo Gabba Gabba for all to be right again with the world.

I believe however you want to mourn is how you should mourn. I have one major theme in all the writings and recordings I've made for Bri on how to deal with my death or the death of any person (or fish): do whatever you need to do to take care of yourself, and you will be okay. In mourning my own imminent death, I've had some pretty crappy days, and I have dealt with them by throwing myself serious pity parties—lots of crying, lying around, more crying, eating, drinking, reality TV, and even more crying. I've also had some pretty amazing days, such as last fall when I laid under the glorious sunshine on the Big "W" at the fifty-yard-line of Camp Randall Stadium, the home of the Badgers, after a very difficult week. Those two coping methods are very different, but they were exactly what I needed at those times. People will always try to give you unsolicited advice on how you should behave when mourning because it's what worked for them. Politely say thank you, and then ignore it. Do what your gut tells you is right for you. And if you have any doubts, seek out a shrink or someone close to you with whom you feel comfortable talking.

The truth is, I don't care if Bri ever watches or reads or listens to anything I've left for her. While it's all been therapeutic for me to compile, it's only there for her if she needs it. If she's still mourning my loss in five or ten or twenty years and wants to hear me sing a song to her or wants to read some of my thoughts, then she'll have all the material waiting for her. But if she's cruising along in life and doesn't need to go back in time to move forward, then she shouldn't pay attention to any of it. And I'm comforted knowing that Jeff will know what to offer her, and when.

My ultimate hope is that by leaving these items for Bri, I will have covered everything tangible she might like to have from me that could help her get through difficult times. Often, when people close to us die, we wish we had one recording, one piece of writing, one memento of some sort that we can hang on to, something that can propel us through a rough day or week or more. And, of course, there's the priceless intangible piece that comes with leaving these things—the fact that Bri will always know how much I loved her and that I am always proud of her.

At four years old, Bri is such an awesome person, so funny and full of joy. I don't want there to ever be a sad cloud lurking over her life. I want her to do whatever she needs to do for herself to be happy. If my absence is what creates a cloud, then maybe some of what I've left behind for her will lift it.

Chapter 12

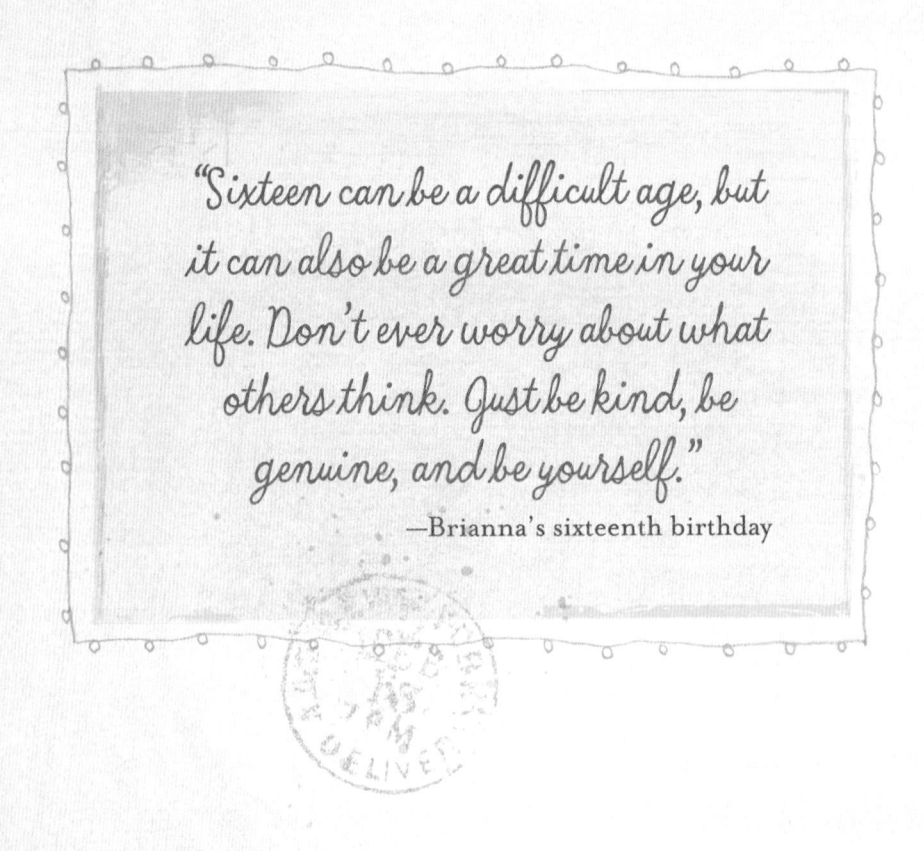

"Sixteen can be a difficult age, but it can also be a great time in your life. Don't ever worry about what others think. Just be kind, be genuine, and be yourself."

—Brianna's sixteenth birthday

Just Be Yourself
BRIANNA'S SIXTEENTH BIRTHDAY

There are two things a young mom with cancer is certain to receive from others: an abundance of opinions on how she should live her life with the disease, and help doing absolutely everything. In my case (and in the case of most metsters), the problem is that sometimes I don't want either one. That's a tough thing to say considering most everyone who provides those things does so out of love. But in those situations, I need to stay true to myself and do what is best for me and my family.

As I've stated, having cancer has brought out the absolute finest in the people around me. My family and I have learned firsthand how much goodness there really is in the world, and we wouldn't be where we are today without the generosity and support we've received. But sometimes, even when people's hearts may be in the right places, they inadvertently overstep boundaries and create more stress in our lives than we currently have. I bring up this topic for one reason: to give those big-hearted, good-willed people a different perspective before they offer unsolicited solutions to someone with cancer, especially someone in stage IV.

About seven months into my cancer treatments and with the hope that I still might beat it, I took the last dose of one of my most despised chemo medications. To celebrate, one of my closest friends bought me a comically enormous box of Nerds candy, my all-time favorite form of sugar. I was so excited about it that I posted a picture of me with the Nerds on social media, then settled in for the evening on the couch to enjoy them with a glass of wine. The next morning, I turned on my computer and was greeted with frantic messages from multiple people. They said they saw my picture with the Nerds (I wondered which of my friends they were referring to until I realized the "N" was capitalized) and were very concerned about me. They asked if I was aware that sugar causes cancer and said I needed to stop eating Nerds immediately to have any hope of winning this battle. How anyone can make something so serious out of a photo of a blue-haired woman gripping a glass of wine and a giant pink-and-purple box with the words "Wonka" and "Nerds" splashed across the front is beyond me, but they did.

I know they meant well, but the last thing I needed after losing both breasts, going through more than a year of horrific treatment, and following every order I was given by doctors was advice from people who had never had cancer, weren't doctors, and probably had no knowledge that Nerds contain the carnauba wax that every human body needs. Okay, so Nerds are nothing but nutritionless pebbles of dextrose, and carnauba wax might not be vital to live. But you know what? Who cares! I know those people were trying to help, but I felt they were insinuating that I wasn't taking care of myself and that I was careless in my effort to get better. I had the Nerds that one time, and nobody can prove that I even ate the whole box! It's kind of like when you're pregnant and everyone thinks your body is automatically up for public discussion and any decision you make is open to judgment simply because your uterus is occupied. ("Really? You're going to eat ... lunch meat?")

Please understand that people in the early stages of cancer have to learn to live with the terrifying reality that even if they are told they are cured, their cancer can return at any time and that it likely will have nothing to do with how they lived during their "cured" time. It's an unbelievably scary thing to deal with, and many people let that fear dictate their lives to the point that they deny themselves the joys of being alive. If the cancer does return, it is because that's what cancer does. It is not because of that extra scoop of ice cream at the mall one Sunday or the can of diet soda now and then. It's also not because I drank out of too many plastic water bottles (someone really said this to someone else about me). Again, I understand in most cases that people mean well, but sometimes good intentions can be very hurtful, especially to someone who's already been through more hurt than most people can imagine.

Since my story about writing cards for Brianna went viral, I've been barraged by emails, at least half a dozen every week, from know-it-alls around the world I've never met who claim to have a cure for my cancer. While it's easy for me to dismiss them as quacks, what's scary is that there are some desperate people with cancer who will try any remedy they read about and ignore evidence-based medicine from the start. It's certainly their right, but by the time they realize it isn't working, it could be too late to try anything else. I have shown to my oncologist some of the treatment suggestions I've received. He told me how dangerous some of those "treatments" can be—in his opinion, more dangerous than chemo, or even cancer itself.

I recently started enthusiastically replying to the people behind some of those emails, congratulating them on finding a cure and telling them I can't wait to tell the nurses at my hospital so they can run around and unplug everyone from their cancer treatments. I ask them for contact information and the pathology for those who were cured because, obviously, they know this advice can kill me if I'm not careful, right? Shockingly, despite being so passive-aggressively nice in my emails, I've never heard back from a single one of them. I guess pouring coffee in my butt (yes, that was one real suggestion) will have to wait until someone provides me with more coffee-butt-based evidence.

I normally don't reply to those who email me because they think they know more than my doctors do. If I'm in a face-to-face situation with a person who tells me her aunt Sally was cured with Hamlin's Wizard Oil (a real thing invented by a magician in the eighteen hundreds who claimed it could kill cancer—again, a magician), I might smile and nod and say thank you for the suggestion because I know they mean well. But what all of us metsters really need is something much simpler: unconditional support. That means without judgment. If a friend is celebrating the last dose of her most-hated chemo by gorging on a box of candy and you can't say "Awesome!" or "I'm happy for you!" or something similar without following your kind words with "but," then it's probably best to stay quiet. Know that it really is our desire to live the highest quality of life we can for as long as we can, and eating handfuls of Nerds one night doesn't mean we're not.

With regard to wanting to physically help someone with cancer—provide meals, do housework, visit them—there is a very simple and polite way to handle it: ask first. That's it—just please ask. This is a tough one because everybody who wants to help does it out of love, and they think anything they do for us is helping, but that's not always the case.

If you want to come over and visit, be it to say hi or to take me to breakfast or to clean around the house, it's very much appreciated, but please understand that I may not want you to at that moment because you may be cutting into my snuggle time with Bri or something else involving her or Jeff that means more to me than anything else in the world. Just ask, and if I say no, don't ever take it personally. Understand that because I'm dying, every bit of my time is prioritized, and nobody will ever rank higher than my family.

If you want to cut our lawn or do some other chore for us, again, ask first. That may sound ridiculous on the surface—how can cutting our lawn be a bad thing? Well, it's not a bad thing at all, but consider this perspective: one of Jeff's few escapes from the chaos of our lives is to be able to go outside and cut the lawn for an hour. It's a chance for him to be by himself, a chance to think—or not to think—with no distractions. It's similar to the staring-out-the-window-to-be-in-the-now thing I do. While so much focus is on me, Jeff's wife is dying. He's going to be a widower soon. Nobody is going through more psychological pain than he is right now, not even me. If you cut the grass without asking, you've done something very nice, but you also may have taken away something Jeff was looking forward to doing for his own mental health.

Unconditional support—that's what metsters need more than anything. I think I also speak for most of us when I say the best way to unconditionally support us is to listen to us. Even in those rare, painful moments when we do open up to you, just stay in that uncomfortable moment with us. Don't worry about saying a thing. We don't expect you to have answers or solutions. Just being there is the most meaningful thing in the world.

Listen to our troubles, listen to our celebrations, listen to what we need, and listen to what we don't need. Then, without judgment, provide us with all the love you can muster.

Chapter 13

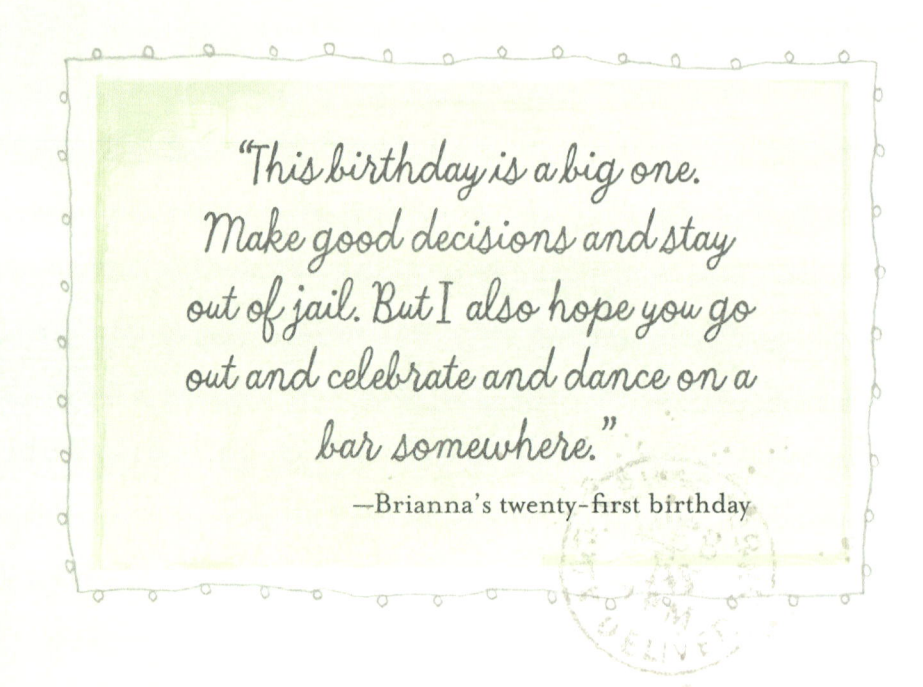

> "This birthday is a big one. Make good decisions and stay out of jail. But I also hope you go out and celebrate and dance on a bar somewhere."
>
> —Brianna's twenty-first birthday

Dance on a Bar Somewhere
Brianna's Twenty-First Birthday

"Scan. Treat. Repeat." That's a common saying we have in the stage IV cancer community. Lovely, isn't it? You get a body part scanned—your brain, your liver, your bones—because it's excruciatingly painful, and you receive some awful treatment for it that can be more miserable than the cancer itself. Then you do it all over again days or weeks later when something else starts to hurt. It's a vicious cycle, physically and psychologically grueling. But I've learned to reduce the mental strain by making one slight addition to that saying:

"Scan. Do something really fun that night like dance on a bar to help you forget you're dying. Treat. Repeat."

I'm proud to say I've danced on many bars, mostly in my pre-Bri days when I was younger, healthy, and could afford to be a little less responsible. I rock out to all kinds of music, never hesitating to express myself. My friend and I even invented a dance move called "The Wall" that took minutes to perfect and includes a dangerous but essential hair flip at the end. For the bald folks in the world, it's more of a brain-rattling head shake—a bit riskier, but I've done it with tremendous success. And if I hear my song "Ice Ice Baby" by Vanilla Ice, shut up and move out of the way. I give that tune everything I have by pretending I've time-warped back to 1990 and I'm dancing around my bedroom putting down some sweet beats. Maybe not as cool as Vanilla, but the effort is there, enough that I at least get a few nods of respect. As an added bonus, I sing. As I've said, I can't hold a tune to save my life, which may be the real reason I'm dying, but that's never stopped me from doing it and having one heck of an awesome time.

While the cancer won't let me move quite like I used to, I still go out and dance with Jeff or my girlfriends when I can, especially on the big, scary scan days or days when I get bad news about something else gone wrong. My reaction after receiving grim results used to be to stay home and wallow in self-pity, worrying about what treatment options the doctors would offer me when I went back to see them the next morning (Option A = Really sucks, Option B = Sucks even worse, Option C = It's best if we just kill you now). But over time, I climbed out of that funk, realizing that no matter what I did after getting hammered with bad news, it wasn't going to change the crap I had to go through the next day. My reality would still be there when I woke up, so why not go out and squeeze in a celebration of life to boost my spirits?

Several years ago, my girlfriends and I started getting together every month or so for Wine Night. I capitalize it because it's a very fancy and serious tradition. When the movie *Magic Mike* came out, we thought it would be a brilliant idea to take Wine Night to another level by holding it in conjunction with the movie. (Yes, it would require us to sneak small purse-size bottles of wine into the theater; you see how fancy and serious this tradition is.) We had a feeling the movie would be so awful that we'd need something more than Milk Duds or yellow-stained popcorn to get us through it. Turned out we were spot-on about the movie. Thanks to the magic of the wine, we had a blast howling at the horrendous acting and "plot" and giggling like twelve-year-old girls whenever Channing Tatum started dancing. (I'm sorry, but that Oscar snub still hurts.) We made the decision right then and there that if there ever was a sequel, we'd go see it and wine would be required.

Fast-forward three years. *Magic Mike XXL* was released, and we were pretty fired up about it. We planned the night well in advance . . . but, of course, I had an oncology appointment earlier that day where I was informed that my chemo, which had seemed to be working well, was no longer doing its job. The doctors were going to discuss later that day what to do next and would have a decision for me in the morning. It was such a blow that I temporarily slipped back into the self-pity mind-set.

"You need to go out tonight," Jeff said after I suggested I might not. "You know there's nothing you can do about this. The doctors don't even know what they're going to do yet. Go have some fun."

I knew he was right, and it didn't require any more convincing than that. Sometimes I just need a swift kick in the butt to remind me that I need to live, especially when the cancer is trying to force me not to.

When the girls and I got to the theater, each with our own wine, we cracked up about how much we'd aged in the three years between movies. For the first movie, we thought nothing of trying to get wine past the ticket-taker guy. But this time around, many of us were dreadfully worried about getting caught. One friend put her small flask of wine under her shirt between her boobs because she was afraid someone would search her purse. Another had two small bottles and made sure to pack them in a way that they wouldn't clink together. A third friend wrote a script of excuses she would use if she was caught. Yeah, she really did that. And then there were two friends who hadn't changed a bit and boldly smuggled in whole bottles of wine—not only an impressive feat, but smart, considering how horrible the film was. We laughed nonstop throughout the movie at its absurdity and had the absolute best time. Surrounded by wine and girlfriends, I definitely give it two thumbs up.

When the movie was over, we went out for some food and dancing and girl talk. One friend with whom I'd already shared the results of my doctor visit asked if I wanted to talk about it. I didn't let my woes dominate our conversations or dull the mood, but I did briefly air my frustrations, and I felt a million times better after doing it. From that talk is where one of my friends suggested starting another meal train, and Jeff and Bri and I were well-fed every night . . . for the next six months! It was a really amazing evening that reminded me how much I was loved, no matter how much the cancer hated me. The next morning, I went back to dealing with my reality, but in a pretty positive frame of mind thanks to the memories of a fantastic evening with the world's best friends . . . and Channing Tatum.

I think the phrase "it is what it is" is often overused, but it's an accurate way to describe stage IV cancer. The cancer in my body is what it is and does what it wants to do. I can't stop it. I can't change it. I can't control it. But one thing it can't stop me from doing is laughing and loving and being loved and celebrating life. And it certainly can't stop me from dancing. I may struggle to hop up on a bar like I used to, but if "Ice Ice Baby" comes on, you'd be foolish to bet against me.

Chapter 14

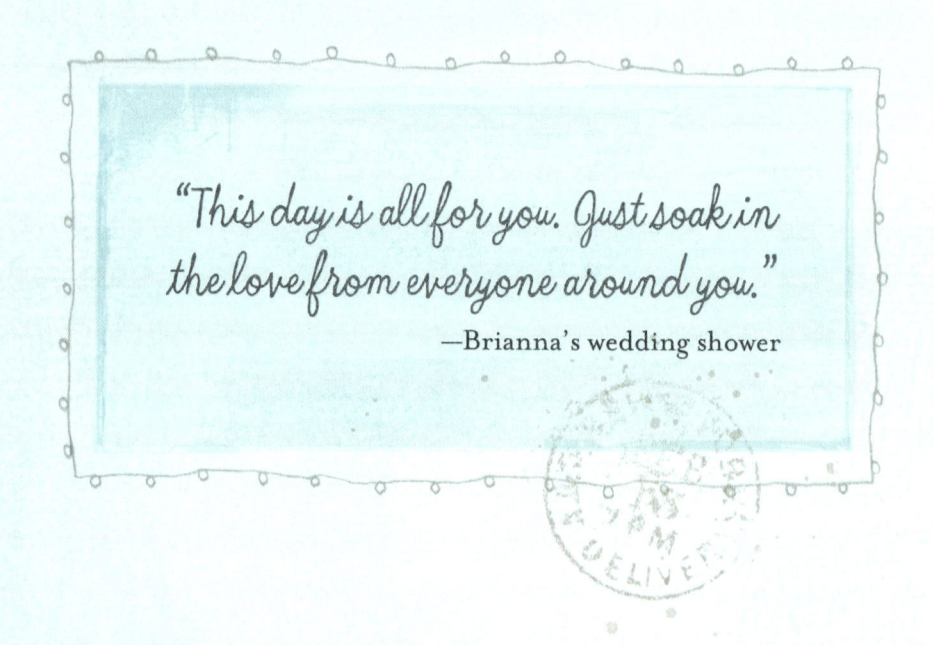

> "This day is all for you. Just soak in the love from everyone around you."
>
> —Brianna's wedding shower

Soak in the Love

BRIANNA'S WEDDING SHOWER

Baldness. It comes with being a cancer patient. You can try to trick yourself into thinking you'll be the one person in the history of chemotherapy not to lose her hair, but that shiny noggin you can't stop ogling in the mirror, car window, lake water, dinner spoon, or the million other places you suddenly realize you can't avoid seeing your reflection will swiftly snap you back to reality.

I grew up with long, luscious brown hair that was a huge part of my identity. It was difficult to accept that it would eventually start falling out in clumps and that, outside of gathering it up and Gorilla-gluing it to my head (very, very, very briefly considered), there was nothing I could do about it.

The only good news I received about losing my hair was that I had time to prepare for it—about three months from the time I was diagnosed. That gave me ample time to mourn its looming death. I gave it a little extra wash, brushed it with a few additional strokes, protected it from the rain, and talked to it. Hey, I was losing a lifelong friend. This was a very big deal. I continued to baby it multiple times each day until I woke up one morning and decided cold turkey that the bereavement period was over. That's when I took control of the situation like only a compulsively organized control freak could: I turned losing my hair into an invitation-only head-shaving party.

I found a salon that graciously agreed to host the event. The date was picked based on when doctors predicted I would start losing hair. I invited about fifteen people who I knew would provide plenty of laughter and love, and we turned it into a lunch party with a bounty of food and wine.

On my way to the salon, I stopped at the grocery store to get a cake. I wanted Bri to witness the event, but I didn't want to traumatize her. The shrink suggested we include her because it would likely be too shocking for her to see her mom walk in the house bald—much better for her to watch the process happen while surrounded by loved ones. It made perfect sense, but I couldn't do it without cake. Bri loves cake. She love loves it. It's not a sweets thing. Candy, ice cream, cookies—those things are fine. But cake is the princess in her sugar world. I think if Bri had to choose between living with Jeff and me or living with cake, she'd at least ask what kind of cake before deciding. And then she'd pick cake.

When I got to the store, all the bakery had was a yellow cake with a black outline smiley face. Not exactly the colorful kind I was looking for, but it would suffice. When I went to check out, the teenage cashier asked me if I was having a party.

"I am," I said.

"What for?" he asked. As you've probably figured out by now, if you ask me an honest question, I'll give you an honest answer.

"Well, I'm going through chemo because I have cancer, and I'm about to lose my hair. So I decided to have a head-shaving party."

He looked at me, taking a moment to digest what I said. I held my breath, hoping his response wouldn't be quite as ignorant as past ones I'd received after bluntly telling people about my disease.

"That's really, really cool!" he said with a smile matching the one on the cake. "That's awesome. Good for you."

Wow! The perfect answer! It was a really nice moment. Even most adults can't handle my frank responses. His reaction couldn't have been better. But then he noticed the port attached to my body, where the chemo is administered.

"Sooo . . . is that where they took the cancer out?"

Waaah . . . waaah . . . waaaaaaah.

He should have taken his prize behind door number one and gone home. But I let it slide. I politely told him what it was for and gave him props for the first response. I truly appreciated it.

The party couldn't have been more fun, considering what it was for. First, the stylist put my hair in a ponytail and cut it off. Ouch! The first snip is always the hardest one to accept. Then she cut some more . . . and some more . . . and some more. You don't realize how much hair you have until you see it falling lifelessly to the floor. But considering I had had long hair all my life, I was quite shocked at how okay I looked as she continued to hack away. When she got it short enough, she pulled out the clippers and finished the job. While comments from the peanut gallery made the entire event bearable and even fun, it was the looks from my friend Morgan, who was sitting behind me throughout the cut, that made me so happy. It seemed the more hair that came off, the more her smile grew.

"I'm getting jealous," she said. "I can't believe how good you look."

The head-shaving party is an example of something else cancer has taught me: sometimes I need to allow some days to be all about me. I don't mean the pity party days by myself locked in a room, but days in which I'm the center of attention being showered with love by others. As much as I enjoy busting a move on the dance floor and going out to have fun, I've never liked when people have been focused on me (remember my public speaking woes?). But there are times when I just need to release control and soak in the love others want to give me to help me get through this disease.

Because of that love, I honestly didn't shed a single tear as my lifelong locks were lopped off. Having time to prepare for it was huge. Having people there who loved me was even bigger. Plus, we had wine. And Bri didn't shed a tear either. In fact, she didn't even flinch at my new look. "It'll grow back, Mommy," she said. Then she had a piece of cake.

Chapter 15

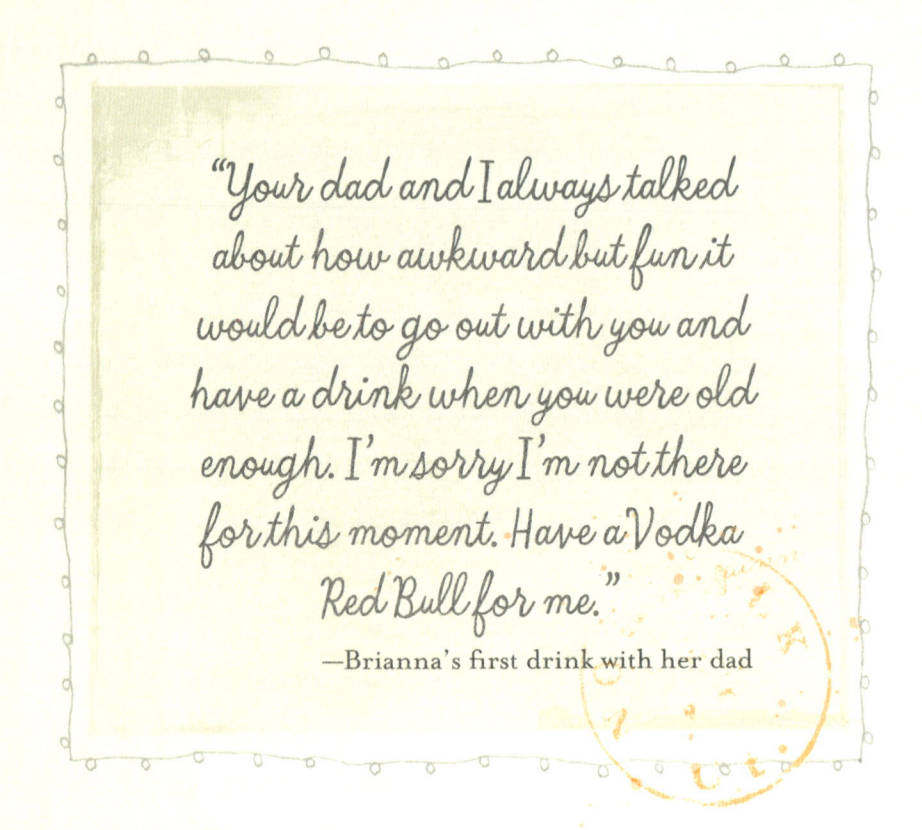

> "Your dad and I always talked about how awkward but fun it would be to go out with you and have a drink when you were old enough. I'm sorry I'm not there for this moment. Have a Vodka Red Bull for me."
>
> —Brianna's first drink with her dad

Say "I Lived"
BRIANNA'S FIRST DRINK WITH HER DAD

One summer day, I went to the cemetery and made the last payment for my final resting place. Unlike my current home, I own the deed to my eternal home free and clear. All that's left for me to do is move in.

I've visited my "spot," as I fondly refer to it, a few times. If that sounds depressing or creepy, well, yeah, I can see that. But I'm cool with it. Seeing where my remains will be in perpetuity is a reality check for when things get tough, a good reminder that I'm not there yet and that I need to continue squeezing every ounce of joy and happiness out of my life while I'm still not urn-sized.

I'm going to be cremated, and with clothes on. Funny story: when the funeral home guy asked me what I'd be wearing for the cremation, I was shocked by the question. I mean, we come into this world naked, so wouldn't we go out that way? It seems so wrong to burn nice clothes. But he was even more blown away that I didn't know that the vast majority of people are clothed during cremation.

"Your body has to be transported in a cremation container," he said incredulously. "You certainly wouldn't go out in public naked, would you?"

I guess it never occurred to me that it was such a big deal. It also seemed slightly strange to be so concerned about clothes, considering the lack of cremation rules there appeared to be otherwise. For example, loved ones are often allowed to throw in various items to be cremated with your body, such as pictures or stuffed animals. Maybe I've discovered an easy way to get rid of the old electronics we have that are so tough to recycle . . .

So, note to anyone who plans to be cremated but has never given it any real thought: naked cremation may not be an option. Put some clothes on. The only directive I gave Jeff was to slip my brand-new, warm, comfy winter coat on me if I died before having the chance to wear it. Since I blew past that milestone when we got our first snowstorm of the season, I'm thinking of going with a UW ensemble or something Mötley Crüe-ish.

My final resting spot is a bit unorthodox. It's a clear glass box built into a wall inside a mausoleum. The box is kind of like a trophy case (insert your own "trophy wife" joke here before Jeff does). My ashes will be placed in an urn, which will be displayed in the box. So when someone walks into the mausoleum, they will be able to see my urn. While most of the spots in the wall are traditional drawers in which a casket slides in and out, my box is stationary in the lower corner of the wall. I made sure to get a spot close to Bri's current height so she can see it. She and Jeff will be able to put things into the box with the urn, such as drawings or messages or pictures. There's room in there for maybe one more urn if anyone wants to join me one day, though I don't ever expect to have company. I assume Bri will be with her future significant other, and Jeff knows I don't want him in there—I want him to find happiness with someone else when I'm gone. So I'm thinking maybe a nice shiny Chicago Bears helmet would look nice.

Most of my neighbors have already moved in, and based on what their loved ones have put in their boxes, they are Green Bay Packers fans. No surprise here in the heart of Wisconsin, though they're going to have to tolerate living forever next to a Bears fan. I know. How is a born-and-raised Wisconsinite a fan of that "other" team? I just am and always have been. Jeff, on the other hand, bleeds green and yellow, and Bri chose to be a Packers fan with him, which means the Bears piece of my legacy will die with me. But I'm okay with that. I'd rather have those two on the same team in every respect when I'm gone.

While I understand the day my urn is placed in the box may be a somber occasion, the service will be anything but that if I have a say in it—which I do. As you know, I love a good party. Combine the resourceful and organized woman in me with the dying party girl, and what do you get? Someone who plans every detail of her own funeral so Jeff doesn't have to worry about it, and to be sure it's a rocking good time for everyone!

The funeral home will handle the cremation but will not host the service. The atmosphere of funeral homes is too traditional and formal for my liking. That's what prompted me to check out Olbrich Botanical Gardens. Olbrich is sixteen acres of breathtaking beauty on the lake in the heart of Madison. Jeff and I had our engagement pictures taken there, and it's a special place for Bri and me. When I took her there the first time, she instantly fell in love with it. It's not a playground or a place designed with bells and whistles to entertain kids. It's a wonderful, peaceful nature walk that fills your senses. I don't know how Bri recognized the value in that at such a young age in a world where kids seemingly have to be constantly entertained by colorful characters or the latest technology, but she did. It's such a big deal to us that we had a plaque installed with our names and the simple words "LOVE THESE GARDENS." Any time Bri asks to go there, I stop what I'm doing to take her.

I picked Olbrich for my service for two reasons. The primary one was for Bri's sake. It's a place where she has fantastic memories of our time together, which should make her feel comfortable, and there will be plenty of places there where she can escape to during the service with any of my friends if she needs to. The second was an incentive they offered when I was there checking out the room they use for private events. The woman showing me around leaned in to me and, in a very classy British accent, whispered the words that sealed the deal: "You can also have a bar." The party was on!

Planning a funeral service is similar to planning your wedding and reception, if you intend for your final good-bye to be festive. You can almost just hand your wedding plan spreadsheet to the funeral director. You need a room, flowers, food, drinks, music. Olbrich provides a projection screen to run a continuous loop of photos. They even asked for a headcount. Seriously? You're going to ask the dying woman how many people she expects to show up for her own funeral? I'm honestly considering creating a Facebook event page for it to see who plans to come.

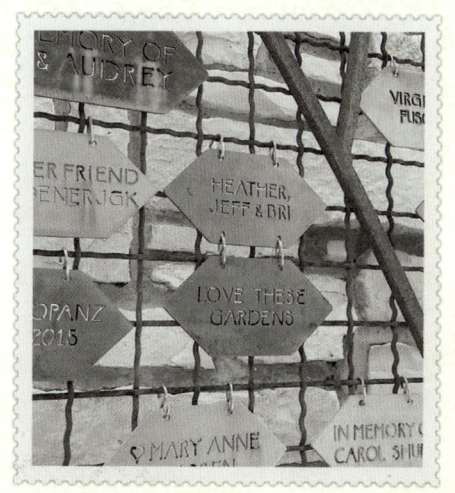

I've planned my party to run for a few hours with an open-house feel to it. People can come and go as they please. The only scheduled event will be a brief reflection that will include a reading and a couple songs. One of the songs will be an all-time favorite of mine: "Keg on My Coffin" by Chris Trapper. If you haven't heard it, it's definitely worth your time…

Put the keg on my coffin

And think of me every so often

Have a losers' day parade

for all my friends

Drink up life like a river

'til the pizza man delivers

And smile and know

I loved you 'til the end

Here's what you do when my time comes to pass

Charlie told me through the reflection

in his glass

Don't waste time praying

'cause I'm never coming back

Just throw a party in my name

Put the keg on my coffin

And think of me every so often

Have a losers' day parade

for all my friends

Drink up life like a river

'til the pizza man delivers

And smile and know

I loved you 'til the end

Here's what to write

on the stone over my grave

His friends were earned,

and not a penny saved

Don't waste time crying

'cause you too are on your way

To meet me at the pawn shop in the sky

Put the keg on my coffin

And think of me every so often

Have a losers' day parade

for all my friends

Drink up life like a river

'til the pizza man delivers

And smile and know

I loved you 'til the end

Smile and know

I loved you 'til the end

Smile and know

I loved you 'til the end

Seriously, if the mood is somber and that song doesn't lighten things up, my friends will need to hit the bar a few more times. All I want is for everyone to have fun enjoying one another's company and swapping stories about me that make their stomachs hurt from laughing so hard. Nobody should be crying unless it's from laughter. I often hear people describe funerals as being a "celebration of life," though I usually find that to be more in theory than truth. The overall mood is generally kind of blah because, well, it's a funeral. But I want mine to truly be a celebration of life. Not only my life, but the lives of those who attend. I crammed a lot of awesome into my brief time here, especially in the last couple of years, thanks to the many wonderful friends I have. I want my death to be an excuse for them to get together and continue that awesomeness with one another.

The other song that will be played is "I Lived" by OneRepublic. I've declared that my official funeral song. Any time I hear it, I turn it up as loud as I can and completely lose myself in it. When people ask me how I want to be remembered in life, I tell them to listen to that song and they'll know.

I wanted to print the lyrics to "I Lived," like I did for "Keg on My Coffin," but I wasn't able to obtain permission to do so before this book needed to be finished (one of the rare times my cancer card failed me). But it's okay that I couldn't, because it gave me a better idea: when you finish this chapter, take a five-minute-and-forty-second break and watch the music video on YouTube. I promise it will be one of the most amazing videos and songs you will ever see and hear, and it will inspire you to push through your trials and live your life to the fullest.

When Bri's old enough to appreciate how great of a song this is, I hope she thinks of me every time she hears it, maybe even offer up a toast to her mom. I did it all, and I want her one day to be able to look back on her life and say she did the same.

(Now go listen to it, but then immediately come back. You still have three chapters and an epilogue to read.)

CHAPTER 16

"You always called your daddy 'Mommy's true love.' I was so incredibly blessed to have met him. Life was infinitely better after that, to have a best friend to laugh and share life with. It's very rare and special to find true love. I'm thrilled beyond words that you have found yours."

—Brianna's wedding

True Love
Brianna's Wedding

Every couple in love has a story of how they came together. Many of those stories are quite fascinating when one considers how many random things had to perfectly align for them to meet each other. The story of Jeff and me began one day during my senior year at the University of Wisconsin. He lived and worked in Madison and was partying before a Badgers game. I was curled up and zoned out on my couch, ready to watch a VH1 documentary on Tupac Shakur and Notorious B.I.G. I'd been at work all day and was exhausted. I was done for the evening—until a friend called and insisted I go to a party with her.

"I'm too tired," I said. "Not tonight. I have to work again tomorrow."

"But you've got to go with me," she implored. "I don't want to go by myself. I promise you'll have a good time."

I wasn't thrilled about it, but I agreed to go. And I'm kind of glad I did, or my last name wouldn't be McManamy.

Jeff and I met at the party. You can call it magical, love at first sight, whatever you want. There was definitely some spark of chemistry there between me and this cute guy wearing a Badgers T-shirt and Texas Longhorns ball cap (his second-favorite college team). We eventually left the party with a group of people and drove randomly around town all night. Sometime during the wee hours, I told Jeff I needed to get home because I had to work at 10:00 a.m.

"Let's keep hanging out," he politely argued. "It's too late to go to sleep now anyways. You'd be more tired when you wake up. I promise I'll get you to work by ten."

Though we'd only known each other for a few hours, I gave him the benefit of the doubt I hadn't given too many guys previously by trusting his word—and he followed through by getting me to work in plenty of time. Hmmm, I thought to myself. A responsible gentleman who does what he says he's going to do? But when we parted ways, there was a problem: he didn't ask for my phone number. That left me in a very perplexed state: I was upset he didn't ask for it, but I was also bothered that I was upset he didn't ask for it.

You see, I didn't have a boyfriend at the time because I didn't want one. It was my senior year. I just wanted to have fun and graduate. No boyfriends. No commitments. No distractions. Plus, I didn't want to risk missing a once-in-a-lifetime job or travel opportunity after graduation because of a guy. Besides, I'd gone out with other guys my previous three years of school, and after a month or two with each one, I was ready to strangle them. I was mainly to blame, not them. I got annoyed at the stupidest things they did. If you were a guy and put butter on your bread at dinner, it would annoy me. If you had to go to the bathroom before we left the restaurant, it would annoy me. I was a real-life *Seinfeld* character. Remember the episode when Jerry broke up with a woman because she ate her peas one at a time? That was me. I wanted a break from all relationships during my last year of college—but Jeff messed up that goal. He was nice. Charming. Handsome. I wanted to be with him. Yes, I knew all that after one night. And the one guy I had felt that way about in years couldn't ask me for my number?

About a week later, I bumped into him downtown, a total chance encounter. I knew the stars weren't going to stay aligned forever, so I told him how I felt.

"Why didn't you ask me out last week?" I said.

"Well, I hesitated at the time because I thought you were out of my league," he replied sheepishly.

Oh, please. The reigning champion of the "Saturday Night Tupac/B.I.G. Documentary League" was out of his league?

"I did finally get the nerve to ask your friend for your number the next day," he continued, "but she wouldn't give it to me because she said you didn't want to be in a relationship."

Touché.

"Well, we should get together," I said casually, offering no explanation for what my friend had told him. I took his cell phone and entered my number in it under the name "Hot Chick." I gave it back, we parted ways, and I waited for his call . . . and waited ... and waited. (Keep in mind, this was prior to social media, so I couldn't even stalk him online. I had no choice but to wait and hope.) As I would later learn, he called the number I put into his phone, but it was the wrong number. Brilliant move, Heather! Just brilliant! The number belonged to some random guy, and Jeff initially wondered if I was living with someone or if I was so darn mean that I would purposely put the wrong number into his phone. Neither was true, of course, and fortunately, he assumed that. He eventually called my friend again, convinced her that I gave him my number but that it was the wrong one, and she gave him my correct number. He finally called, we went out several times after that, and six months later, I recognized a breakthrough in my maturity level:

"Oh my gosh, I don't want to strangle you!" I said. "I find nothing about you that's annoying."

Yes, I really said that to him. Not the most flattering compliment, but he knew my experiences with other guys. The love between Jeff and me was there, and we both embraced it. Our relationship flourished during my senior year, we dated for a few years after that, and we married in 2006.

And if you look at Jeff's cell phone today, I'm still in there under "Hot Chick."

In May 2016, we will celebrate our tenth wedding anniversary. Along with Bri's fifth birthday a month earlier, there is no bigger milestone I want to reach. But Jeff and I both know that may not happen. There's nothing we can do about it, and it absolutely breaks my heart. This isn't fair to either of us, especially Jeff, the one being left behind.

I've been told repeatedly by my oncologists that this cancer is not my fault. I know it's not. My lemon of a body was destined for this fate, and nothing could have changed it. It's been in the repair shop more times than I can count, and everything that could possibly be done to fix it has been done. But I still feel like I'm the one doing this to Jeff—and that hurts a ton. All I've ever wanted in our relationship is for him to be as happy as he can be, and now I'm about to make him as sad as he can be. I know fairy-tale endings are rare. Heck, I've noticed even in many of the classic Disney movies I've watched with Bri that the mother is killed off: *Bambi*, *The Fox and the Hound*, *The Little Mermaid*, *Finding Nemo*, and Bri's favorite, *Frozen*. Kids and/or spouses are left behind, deeply shadowed with grief. The movies, in that sense, are a true reflection of life. But why do some people live to be a hundred and others don't make it more than a day? Why does someone with a disease get cured, while another person with the same disease doesn't? Why do good people die before bad people?

We all have our own beliefs about death. I've become comfortable accepting the randomness of the universe. If someone was standing three feet to the right, they wouldn't have been hit and killed by that car. If someone had left their house ten seconds earlier, they wouldn't have been in that accident. If their pathology had been slightly different . . .

But I also see the many awesome and amazing things that happen because of that same randomness. What if cancer had invaded my body when I was a teenager and

I didn't live long enough to meet Jeff? And if I hadn't met Jeff, then Bri wouldn't be here. As often as I denounce the unfairness of my situation, I realize how lucky I am to have had the thirty-six-plus wonderful years I've had. A lot of people don't get close to that age or get to experience everything I've packed into my life.

But it still hurts to think about the agony Jeff is going to suffer when I'm gone and that my cancer is going to be the cause of that pain.

I naturally receive sympathy from people when they find out I'm dying. I truly appreciate it, more than I can ever express. But the fact is I've got the easy way out. Once I'm gone, I'm gone. It's Jeff who will have to find a way to push through the emotional distress, to raise Bri, and to do it all without his soul mate. I've thought a lot lately about how difficult it must be for a widow or widower after a funeral. Everyone goes home after the service, back to their normal lives, and the grieving spouse is left to try to figure out how to live after being accustomed to being with the same person, often their best friend, for years or even decades. That's the reality that is about to hit Jeff. That's the reality I've struggled with.

When a person dies, some people like to send flowers or donate money to the family. That's always appreciated, and I wouldn't tell anyone not to do that for my family if that's what they want to do. But for anyone who would like to do something in my memory that's outside the box, think about someone you know who is a widow or widower—a parent, grandparent, sibling, neighbor, coworker. Then do something nice for that person that lets them know you're thinking of them. It doesn't matter how long they've been alone, because I doubt the pain of losing a spouse ever goes away. Your gesture may only be a drop or two in the vast emptiness in their heart, but a drop or two repeatedly, or from many people, can add up. Take them to lunch, call them and talk for a few minutes, pay them a visit, offer to do some odd jobs for them, or, as I've been known to do on occasion, send them a card with a warm, handwritten note inside.

Yes, a card is always good.

Chapter 17

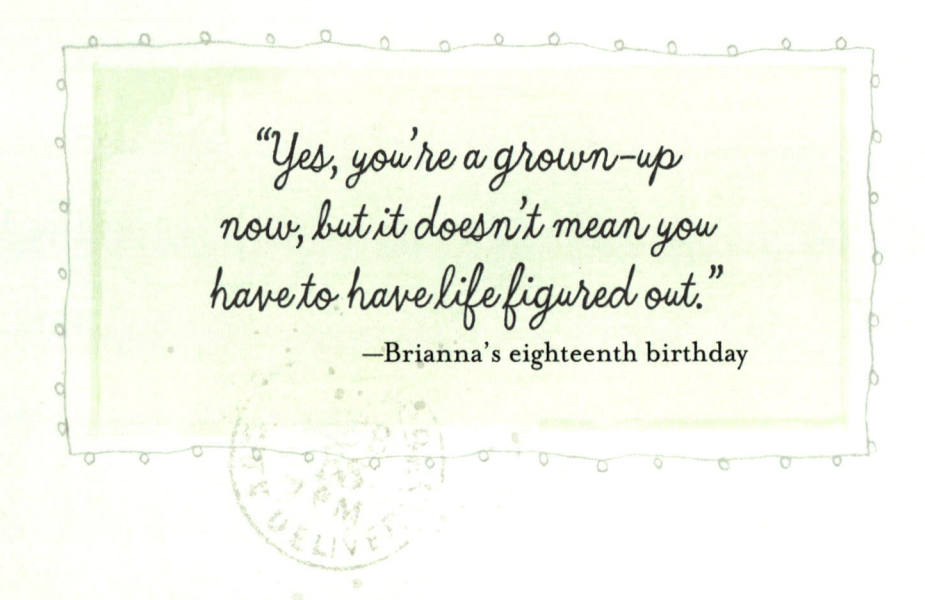

> "Yes, you're a grown-up now, but it doesn't mean you have to have life figured out."
>
> —Brianna's eighteenth birthday

Explaining the Unexplainable
Brianna's Eighteenth Birthday

About the time when we found out my cancer had spread to my liver, our golden retriever, Mitzie, died of cancer. She was our best friend, full of unconditional love. It pained us to have to tell Bri, who was just three, that Mitzie was gone. I did a massive amount of research and consulting with others about how to share such sad news with a child so young, and we determined the best way to do it was to be as black-and-white about it as possible: tell her what happened in a very consistent and honest way, let her process it, and see how she would react. So we did. We sat Bri down in the grass and told her Mitzie had been sick and died, we turned her body into dust, she wasn't coming back, and we would still love Mitzie even though she was gone. Bri stared at us, wiggled her lower lip a tad, asked if she could play on her swing, smiled when we said yes, and ran off.

A few weeks later, I took Bri to get a haircut. The hair stylist struck up a conversation with Bri by asking her if she had any pets.

Uh-oh.

My heart pounded hard as I nervously awaited Bri's response. My research didn't include anything about the possibility of spontaneous questions from a hair stylist. This was going to be a good test.

"I had a dog named Mitzie," Bri said, "but she died."

"Oh, I'm sorry to hear that," the woman replied.

"Her body stopped working, and she's never coming back," Bri continued with authority.

The woman looked at me, horrified.

"So is Mitzie in heaven?" she asked.

"No," Bri said. "Her body turned to dust and she's dead and she's never coming back."

I guess it's safe to say Bri handled Mitzie's death pretty well emotionally, and with the clear understanding we'd hoped for.

While we told Bri about Mitzie in frank terms, I believe there's an abundance of gray area as far as how to properly handle situations like this with children. There is no one right way or one wrong way to do it. What is right for my child may not be right for yours. The age of the child certainly matters. Your culture matters. I'd love if there were one set of sure-fire rules that would work for every kid of every age and background when it comes to talking about the death of a loved one, but there isn't.

So how do we tell a four-year-old girl that her mother is dying? Well, we haven't yet, but we're gradually getting there. I have one primary job as a mom: not to die before my child grows up. It is the most horrific, awful, terrifying thing in the world to know I will not be able to keep my end of that bargain and that we somehow have to tell Bri that I can't. But I'm a planner, so it should come as no surprise that we have a plan in motion to handle this very delicate situation. Through an abundance of reading, a lot of conversations with widows and widowers of friends of mine who have died from cancer, and consistent sessions with the child psychiatrist (some that have included Bri), everything is unfolding in due time. Our goal is to make my actual death as seamless for Bri as possible. We know it won't be perfectly seamless, but "as seamless as we can make it" is a good goal to have.

We haven't come right out and told her what's happening to me because at her age, she will likely wake up each day thinking that's the day I'm going away forever, and we don't want to traumatize her. Even telling her it may happen in a week or a month or a few months probably won't make a lot of sense to her; kids live in the moment and don't have the same concept of time as adults. The Mitzie-black-and-white approach would not be a good idea in this situation. What we're doing is letting Bri guide a lot of the conversation by answering her questions and trying not to hide too much from her. We introduce some things later than others, but so far, everything is going according to plan.

She knows I'm sick—that can't be hidden, and we don't want to hide it. She sees me take medications, she knows I have to go to the doctor for treatments, she knows I can't have dance parties with her for as long as I used to or that I might not be able to go to the mall because the cancer makes me so tired. Seeing me slowly decline will be better for her than hiding it all and then shocking her one day with my death.

The older Bri gets, the more and more questions she has about the cancer, and we answer them honestly. She hasn't connected the dots yet to ask "What happens if doctors can't get rid of the cancer?" Questions out of a four-year-old's mouth generally come randomly and in rapid succession: "Mommy, why is the sky blue? Why is a car called a car? Do we have any cookies? Are you going to die? Why do dogs bark?" If she eventually does put two and two together, we'll answer the question the best and most candid way we can without mortifying her, as we have done with all of her inquiries the past couple of years.

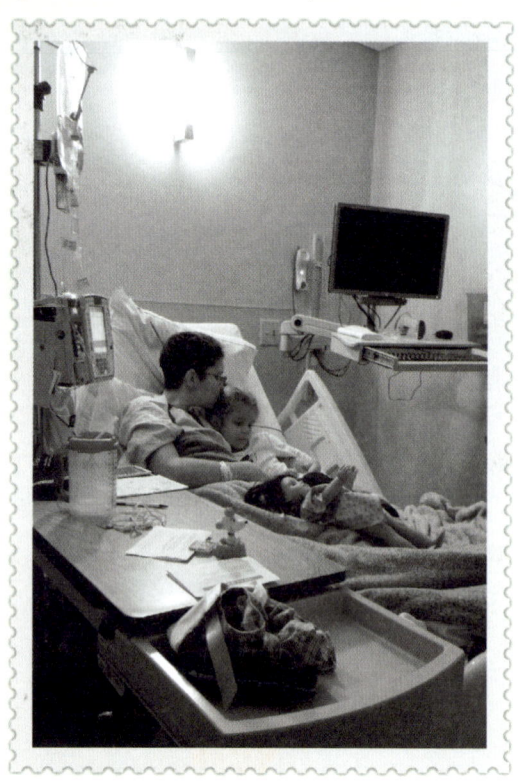

We progressed a little further last fall when I had to check into the hospital for a procedure. I had to spend a couple nights there, so we decided to bring Bri to the hospital for the first time. We'd never exposed her to that environment before because a hospital can be a scary and overwhelming place for a kid. But with a lot of preparation and the fantastic medical staff, we made it a very inviting experience for her. The nurses fawned over her. We held dance parties and sang. We watched *Mickey Mouse Clubhouse*. We read books in bed. Before Bri went home each night, she gave me one of her dolls so I wouldn't be alone. Everything that happens to me as a result of the cancer is normally a shock to us the first time or two, but it ultimately becomes a new normal. To an extent, we normalized the hospital for Bri with those November visits.

About a month after that, I got my own wheelchair, and Bri was absolutely freaking excited! A week earlier, before I had the chair, we were all supposed to go to the mall to see Santa Claus and do some shopping, but my body was not cooperating. While I stayed home and had one of my emotional breakdowns because I couldn't go, Jeff and Bri went to the mall on their own. So when Bri saw the new wheelchair the following week, she didn't see it as something negative; quite the contrary, in fact. She saw it as "Now you can go with us and do things, Mommy!" When we went on a spectacular weekend getaway to Miami thanks to the wonderful people at the Jack & Jill Late Stage Cancer Foundation, I had to use a wheelchair to get through the airports, so Bri knew when I got one at home how much good it could provide me. I think the chair has been a beautiful lesson for her: it's okay to ask for help when you need it, and when you receive that help, sometimes your day and the day for those around you can become a little bit brighter.

One thing we won't do with Bri, which we also didn't do when Mitzie died, is tell her that I'm going to heaven. Some people may object to that, and I understand; it's not an easy topic to address. What we feel we need to consider most with this issue, which our psychiatrist and widows and widowers with young children have helped us with immensely, is how the mind of a child works. When a child this young is told that Mommy is somewhere else, even heaven, the natural reaction of that child is to think Mommy would rather be in that other place, that Mommy is choosing to be there rather than to be here with her child. A child as young as Bri may not necessarily be comforted with the thought of there being a heaven in the same way an adult would be because she may be too young to understand it. Again, she thinks in black-and-white: "Mommy is not here, Mommy is somewhere else, and therefore, Mommy would rather be there than with me." She may also have the false hope that, since Mommy chose heaven over her, Mommy might change her mind one day and come back. If Bri were older, our explanation might be different. And as she gets older and forms her own beliefs, Jeff will certainly support her.

What we want Bri to understand unequivocally right now is that my body stopped working and I'm no longer in pain. We also want her to know that while I may not be here anymore, there is absolutely no place I'd rather be than with her. Our deepest hope is that with a combination of that explanation, everything we've gradually revealed to her so far about my condition, and the incredible support group she will have surrounding her, Bri will be able to not only psychologically "get through" my death, but also flourish in life now and in the future. I don't expect her to ever be able to figure out the "why" with regard to my passing. It's one of those things in life that none of us understand. I just want her to grow up with the comfort of knowing that I loved her to pieces, still love her to pieces, and will always love her to pieces, no matter where I am.

Chapter 18

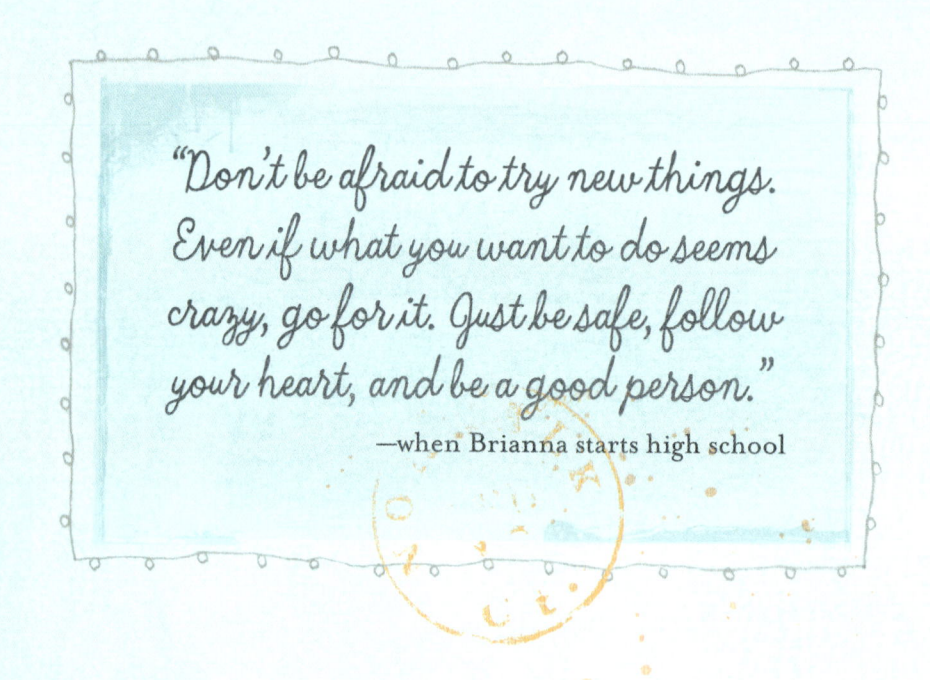

> "Don't be afraid to try new things. Even if what you want to do seems crazy, go for it. Just be safe, follow your heart, and be a good person."
>
> —when Brianna starts high school

Follow Your Heart
When Brianna Starts High School

I've always had healthy fear of trying new things, but I've never let that stop me from doing them. Even before the cancer, I was adventurous. Maybe not quite to the extent that I have been since I was terminally diagnosed, but I've always believed that to experience is to live. Take this book, for example. Many people in my position might have said, "I'm dying. How can I even think of writing a book?" But my thought was, "I'm dying. Why not try to write a book?" Instead of feeling sorry for myself while some Red Devil is being infused into my vein, why not use that time to record my feelings about it? Plus, the thought of being able to add "author" to my obituary and, of course, to that braggy accomplishment page in my alumni magazine is pretty cool.

I could probably write four or five books considering all the stories I have about living with cancer. It's always something new every day, sometimes every hour. Since time is sort of an issue for me, I had to limit myself to one book, but I want to use this chapter to share some vignettes that I thought were too beautiful or funny or absurd not to include . . .

Bucky Badger

Taylor Mehlhaff, a friend and former kicker for the Badgers, arranged for us to tour Camp Randall Stadium and meet some of the football players. Bri was so fired up to meet their mascot, Bucky, whom she'd seen many times on television. I mean, she was super jacked up about it! She used to be afraid of Bucky, but she said she wasn't anymore. She said they were going to dance and "Jump Around," a reference to the song that's played before the fourth quarter of each home football game. She was pumped! This was the day she and Bucky were going to become best friends!

But after we got to the stadium, while standing outside the team offices, Bucky shot out from behind a wall and . . .

Oh . . . dear . . . God.

Bucky scared the crap and then some out of Bri. When Bri gets nervous, she doesn't scream or cry. She has a panic attack. Her body shakes uncontrollably. Her knees lock. Her fingers go into her mouth. And her words become one very long word: "HiBuckyHiBuckyIGottaGoIGottaGoHiBuckyByeBuckyIGottaGo—" She finally went, dashing into the nearby trophy room and slamming the door behind her—the same trophy room where just a few minutes earlier, she'd said to the staff, "You guys need more trophies." To get her to come out, I had to convince her that security had Bucky removed from the stadium for the rest of the day.

Fortunately, the day got better—way better. We got to walk on the field, go into the locker rooms and players' lounge, and meet the coaches and players. The amount of time everyone spent with us was beyond generous. The players invited Bri into their practice huddle and truly made her their friend. She gave every one of them a hug and made sure to tell them she takes her Flintstones vitamin every day so she can grow up to be healthy and strong like them. About a week later, I was blown away when she received a card from those same players who said they'd try to win more trophies and make the other teams' mascots sad. I also received a letter from the players that said how much my situation and positive attitude taught them to soak in the moment on the field each game and appreciate the opportunities they have. I sensed my presence had an impact when they saw Jeff and me reading a sign posted in their locker room that says "Every Day Matters." They knew what that sign meant to me, which gave it an entirely new meaning to them. It was an incredible day for a lot of people. And I'm also happy to say that Bri is a fan of Bucky once again . . . on TV.

"You are shedding ikva amazinh"

"You are shedding ikva amazinh"

Fentanyl is like morphine, but a heck of a lot stronger. I call it my "happy juice," a medication I take for conscious sedation before a procedure. It really does make me feel incredibly happy. But there's a problem (well, to Jeff it's a problem, not to me): when it's being administered, all I want to do is text. It's become habit. The fentanyl goes in, and my hand instantly reaches for my phone. Jeff constantly tries to take the phone from me, but I refuse to give it to him. For some reason, lying in the hospital while getting fentanyl is one of the rare times I feel like a true cancer patient. (Weird, right?) I think clinging to my phone and having a link to the outside world is a way to hang on to my normal. Yes, even when passing out and dropping the phone on my face. Repeatedly. Each text takes me at least fifteen minutes to type and send. Jeff can only watch painfully, hoping the phone will die. I insist it's okay that I do it because I always assume (incorrectly) that autocorrect will help me. When I pass out and Jeff tries to snatch the phone away, I pop up and snag it back. I'll put up a fight if I have to. My friends have become used to my texts and know when they are fentanyl-induced. This was one of my brief but legendary fentanyl texting conversations:

Me: "Face can't read."

Me: "Dave guy did the b8id poi that did my initial nerrir core biopsy. I have conme go bottle"

Friend: "Come full circle! I can read fentanyl talk!!!!"

Me: "ShavingYou Arlo"

Me: "You are GDP r are ewe I jeez"

Me: "You are shedding ikva amazinh"

Friend: "Thank you."

If you're dying and ever have to take fentanyl, I recommend you have your phone with you. Jeff and others would say that's the opposite of the advice I should give, but remember that laughter, which fentanyl and I have harmlessly provided for many of my friends, is the best medicine. If you're not dying and have to take fentanyl, you may want to refrain from texting since you probably don't want to send babbling texts to your boss or someone else important. Though even then, it might be kind of funny.

Bad breakup?

I'm sensitive about telling people I'm terminal because I know not everyone can handle it. Rarely do I reveal my condition during everyday encounters unless someone asks . . . or pushes me so far that they leave me no choice but to tell them.

I was at a bar one night with my friend Kate (the one who said I suck at cloud watching) when "I Lived" started playing. Sitting in a bar at the end of the evening and my funeral song comes on? Not a good concoction, especially when it was the same day I discovered my current chemo drug was no longer working and I was one huge step closer to my funeral. I looked at Kate with tears welling in my eyes, shrugged hopelessly as if to say "There's nothing anyone can do to make this better right now" and went to compose myself in the bathroom as any grown-up would.

Kate stayed at the table. It was pretty late, and only a handful of college students remained. They were milling around making awkward eye contact with Kate, one half probably debating whether they should flirt with her and the other half wanting to know more about her teary-eyed friend. Finally, the silence was awkwardly broken when a girl nodded in Kate's direction and asked, "Bad breakup for your friend?"

"Nope," Kate said plainly. "Stage IV terminal cancer. She's dying."

Hey, one perk of having a friend with terminal cancer is that you can have some fun playing the cancer card every now and then. The girl and her friends stared in stunned silence. When I came back and sat down, they darted straight for the door without saying a word. I don't know if they thought cancer was contagious or if they just didn't know what to say. This was also at a time when I happened to have a full head of hair and looked healthy, probably making Kate's revelation even more shocking to them. There was nothing wrong with the girl asking Kate if I was upset over a breakup—she may have cared or, at the very least, was making casual conversation. But maybe there's a good lesson in this: don't assume you know someone's story, and don't ask if you think you may not be able to handle the truth.

Another time, I was having a horrible day, feeling physically awful after chemo, when I realized I was out of contact lenses. I went to a local chain store that was able to see me right away. I explained that my prescription was the same, I needed a quick exam, and I wanted however many contacts my insurance would cover.

When it came time to pay, they told me insurance would cover six months' worth of lenses. Perfect. I told them I'd take that. But they refused to listen, insisting I get a year's worth. I was incredibly polite, especially for as bad as I felt. I said "No, thank you, I just need the six month supply please" multiple times. I know they had a job to do, but nobody would listen to me . . . and then it started getting personal.

"But this isn't a smart decision," the lady said. "You're throwing money away by not getting at least a year of lenses. Let me explain again. You're paying more. Jim, come over here. Look at what she wants to do. This isn't a smart choice, is it? She's wasting money."

That was my breaking point.

"Look," I said with a gigantic smile. "I'm terminally ill. I will be dead in a year. Seriously. And I'm pretty sure I do not need contacts when I'm dead. Please give me the amount the insurance covers so I can go home."

There was a looong awkward silence. They didn't say another word, gave me my contacts, and I went on my way. I cringed at what I said the entire way home. I'd never done that out of frustration to anyone. I felt bad. But over time, I've come to embrace the attitude of "You want to ask or not listen to me? Be prepared for my response." Sometimes you should take no for an answer. I don't think even the world's best salesperson could sell contact lenses to a dead person. And, for the record, I still have almost a box of those contacts left. One of my last goals in life is not to use one pair more than I bought that day.

Another quick bar story

One of my dearest friends, Jen, has often come to sit with me during my chemo treatments. Back in my pre-cancer days, when we frequented bars, we'd make a lap of the bar when we got our first drink. You know, to feel up the lay of the land, check out the clientele, see if there's a good spot to do "The Wall." After a few chemo visits, we realized old habits die hard—Jen and I still do the lap! We get our drink, grab my IV pole, and make a social circle to scope out what's going on and to see who's there. Now that I visualize this, it may explain why, since the pole joined us, they've started seating us in the way, waaay back section . . .

And a quick bald story

More of an observation than a story, I guess. The first time you're bald and you go out in the rain in the summer and take your hat off and slowly stroll through the downpour without a care in the world is one of the most glorious moments you will ever experience. It's a close second to the first time you get to feel the wind blowing through your hair again once it starts to grow back. Even if you're naturally bald, give it a try the next time it rains. You'll feel what I mean.

Happy Birthgivingmas New Year!

    The week of Thanksgiving last year, a couple of my friends took me to my first experience with palliative spinal radiation for bone metastases, a fancy way of saying, "We can't fix the massive amount of cancer in your bones causing your unrelenting pain, but maybe we can make it hurt a tad less after making it hurt much worse for a week or two." When we got home, I was exhausted, sick, and in terrible pain. Determined to celebrate every big day coming up (just in case), we had cake, sparkling grape juice, sang songs, blew out candles, counted down the New Year, and celebrated Christmas, all while I was immobilized and tucked under a blanket in my chair. They then performed a scene from one of my favorite TV shows, *Friday Night Lights,* in costume and in character. I've never laughed so hard in my life. Every cackle hurt a ton, but it was pain I was more than happy to endure.

    Rather than dropping me off at home and running out the door, too afraid to see the side effects of radiation, they stayed to make me smile and laugh and just be normal friends having fun. We were being silly in ways we never would have unless I were in that condition. It was so awesome. These are two of the many friends I'm trusting to help Jeff raise Bri. Now you see why I'm not worried?

Arm Spanx

When you have lymph nodes removed, you become at risk for lymphedema. This means your arms can swell up super huge, maybe forever. I'm missing thirteen nodes. (Only one was positive for about a millimeter of cancer, but they "got it all out" because I caught it early and since I was "relatively thin" and my lymph nodes were fairly clumped together, they scraped out a whole bunch because, well, better safe than sorry, right?) Because I'm missing so many, the fluid doesn't circulate like it should. Usually, it will compensate and be fine. But sometimes infections or bug bites or, for whatever weird reason, flying can trigger lymphedema. With a ton of physical therapy it could go away, but it still really sucks.

So I have this arm compression sleeve I wear when I fly. I was struggling with it in the airport bathroom on the way to Disney when I noticed a very sweet-looking twenty-something woman staring at me. I didn't know what she was going to say, but I was afraid it would be something that would require me to reveal my terminal diagnosis. I was mentally preparing an answer.

"Um, excuse me? Is that arm Spanx you're wearing?" she asked.

"Huh?" This was a new one.

"You know, Spanx, but for your arm?" she said. "Because let me tell you, honey, your arms look just fine in that shirt. You certainly don't need the Spanx!"

It took me a second, but I realized she thought I was putting the sleeve on because I thought my arms looked fat in my shirt. I laughed and explained what it was for.

"Oh, okay, that makes sense," she kindly replied. "Because you look good!"

What a wonderful and unexpected compliment from a stranger. People often have no idea what a random compliment can do for someone, cancer or not, even when it requires saying the phrase "arm Spanx."

What is that?

I had reconstructive surgery after my double mastectomy, but once I was in stage IV, I decided I was done with elective procedures. I'm fine with my scars, but I wasn't sure how Bri would react when she saw how different my body was compared to hers. Until I could think of how I wanted to word the explanation, I figured I'd be discreet while showering or changing around her.

But one day in the bathroom, she caught me.

"Mama! What is that?" she screamed with horror.

I had been putting on deodorant and didn't realize my towel had partially fallen down. Of course, I panicked. I wasn't ready! This was it! The big moment! I was going to have to be supermom and somehow say the perfect thing! But I froze. So I tried to stall. I pulled up the towel and asked what she meant.

"That, Mama! That! What is that? Why do you have it?"

She was completely disgusted. But she wasn't pointing at my scars. She was pointing at the stick of deodorant! She'd never noticed me putting it on before. I clarified that's what she was asking about. When she nodded, I answered her question.

"That's gross," she calmly said and walked out of the bathroom.

It proved, yet again, how resilient kids are. She didn't notice the massive scars across my chest or the fact that I didn't have nipples. Just like when I was bald, all she saw was Mom . . . which is a pretty beautiful thing.

·EPILOGUE·

"Sometimes it will seem like things are not okay and never will be, but the fact that you're even here to experience those things not being okay is enough to hang on to a little bit of hope. Sometimes bad things end up working out pretty well. Through all the crap I dealt with, I always found silver linings. Take the time to look for them."

—a card for hope

Every Day Matters
Heather's Final Goodbye

Heather McManamy

December 15, 2015 · McFarland, WI, United States

Hello all, I am posting this on behalf of the love of my life. These are her words. Much love to all. – Jeff McManamy

So . . . I have some good news and some bad news. The bad news is, apparently, I'm dead. Good news, if you're reading this, is that you are most definitely not (unless they have wifi in the afterlife). Yes, this sucks. It sucks beyond words, but I'm just so damn glad I lived a life so full of love, joy and amazing friends. I am lucky to honestly say that I have zero regrets and I spent every ounce of energy I had living life to the fullest. I love you all and thank you for this awesome life.

Please, please, please do not tell Brianna that I am in heaven. In her mind, that means that I chose to be somewhere else and left her. In reality, I did everything I could to be here with her, as there is nowhere, NOWHERE, I would rather be than with her and Jeff. Please don't confuse her and let her think for one second that is not true. Because, I am not in heaven. I'm here. But no longer in the crappy body that turned against me. My energy, my love, my laughter, those incredible memories, it's all here with you. Please don't think of me with pity or sadness. Smile, knowing that we had a blast together and that time was AMAZING.

More than anything, I love making people laugh and smile, so please, rather than dwelling on the tragic *Terms of Endearment* end of my story, laugh at the memories we made and the fun we had. Please tell Brianna stories, so she knows how much I love her and how proud of her I will always be (and make me sound waaay cooler than I am). Because I love nothing more than being her mommy. Nothing. Every moment with her was a happiness I couldn't even imagine until she came crashing into our world.

And don't say I lost to cancer. Because cancer may have taken almost everything from me, but it never took my love or my hope or my joy. It wasn't a "battle," it was just life, which is often brutally random and unfair, and that's simply how it goes sometimes. I didn't lose, dammit. The way I lived for years with cancer is something I consider a pretty big victory. Please remember that.

Most importantly, I was unbelievably lucky to spend over a decade with the love of my life and my best friend, Jeff. True love and soulmates do exist. Every day was full of hilarity and love with Jeff by my side. He is genuinely the best husband in the universe. Through all my cancer crap, he never wavered when so many people would want to run. Even on the worst days you could imagine, we found a way to laugh together. I love him more than life itself and I truly believe that a love like that is so special it will live forever. Time is the most precious thing in this world and to have shared my life for so long with Jeff is something I am incredibly grateful for. I love you, Jeff. I believe that the awesomeness that is Brianna is our love brought to life, which is pretty beautiful. It absolutely breaks my heart to have to say goodbye. If it's half as sad for you as it is for me, it breaks my heart over again because the last thing I ever want to do is make you sad. I hope that with time, you can think of me and smile and laugh, because, holy shit did we have a breathtaking life. Go Google Physicist's Eulogy and know that it is a scientific fact I will always be with you both in some way. I know that if you just stop and look hard enough, I'll be there (in as non-creepy a way possible). You're my world and I loved every second we had together more than words.

Friends, I love you all and thank you for the most wonderfully awe-inspiring life. And thank you to all of my amazing doctors and nurses who have taken such incredible care of me. I don't doubt that my team gave me every possible good day that they could. From the bottom of my heart, I wish all my friends long, healthy lives and I hope you can experience the same appreciation for the gift of each day that I did. If you go to my funeral, please run up a bar tab that would make me proud. Heck, blast "Keg on My Coffin" and dance on the bar for me (because there had better be a dance party at some point). Celebrate the beauty of life with a kickass party because you know that's what I want and I believe that in a weird way, I will find a way to be there too (you know how much I hate missing out on fun). I look forward to haunting each one of you, so this isn't so much a good-bye as it is see you later. Please do me a favor and take a few minutes each day to acknowledge the fragile adventure that is this crazy life. Don't ever forget: every day matters.

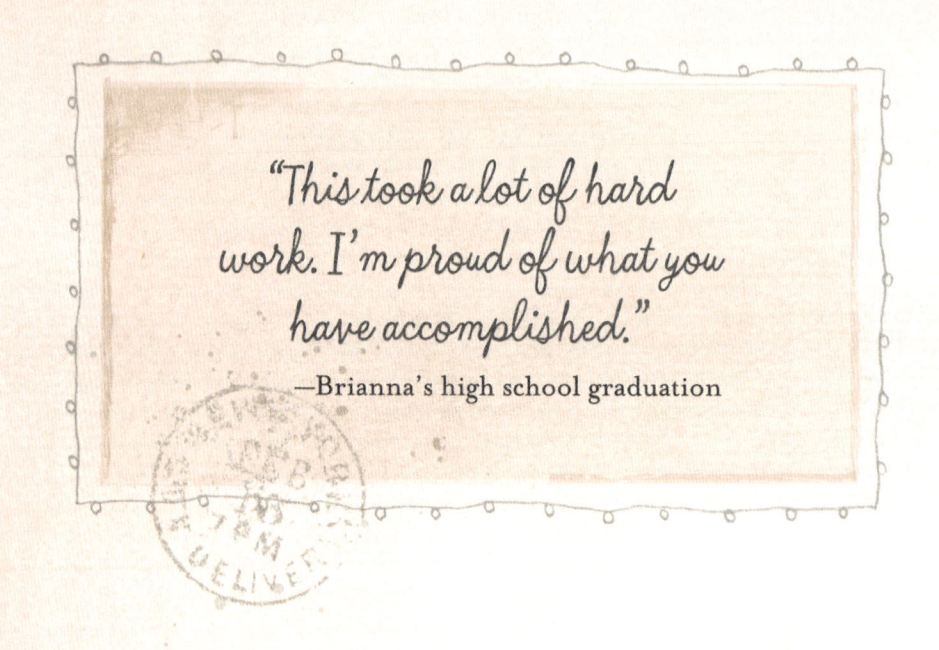

"This took a lot of hard work. I'm proud of what you have accomplished."

—Brianna's high school graduation

Acknowledgements

Thank you to the countless friends and family who have held our hands and have helped turn the most terrifying past few years of our young lives into the most joyful and beautiful ones. Your unconditional support and genuine love have carried us through the scariest of days, helping us realize that no matter what happens, everything will be okay. And thank you for the laughter and the love and the memories that keep us smiling at times when it doesn't seem possible.

Thank you, William Croyle, for stalking me in the most professional of ways and bringing one of my dreams to life. I never could have imagined my final months would be spent focused on such a beautiful and meaningful project. From beginning to end, this has been one of the most fun, rewarding, and enjoyable ventures I have ever had the pleasure of working on. To be able to team up with you has been an absolute treat (despite your taste in football teams). You are truly a gifted writer, and my family will always cherish your hard work in telling our family's story so genuinely and honestly. Most of all, thanks for the laughter.

Thank you to my incredible healthcare team that fought for me to be able to live every possible minute on this earth with my family. I don't doubt for one second that I have received the best care in the world. I am beyond lucky to have zero regrets regarding treatment. People call me an inspiration. I simply show up and agree to let you do things to me. Thank you for fighting on my behalf. You are the real heroes.

Thank you to Ronald Goldfarb and Gerrie Sturman with Goldfarb and Associates; Anna Michels, Liz Kelsch, Valerie Pierce, and Sara Hartman-Seeskin with Sourcebooks; and Nichole Stewart and Delia Berrigan Fakis with Hallmark. Not everybody believed in this project, but you all did from day one. My family and I are forever grateful to you and all those who worked with you behind the scenes for making this come to fruition.

Thank you to our friends and family who had a hand in the development of the manuscript, helping us to prepare and polish it for publication: Jeff McManamy, Morgan McCoy, Jen Dickman, Debra Croyle, Judy Jakyma, and Lisa Kovach. Your words of wisdom were invaluable in making this a success.

And thank you to every person across America and around the world who has ever messaged me, tagged me, liked me, friended me, poked me, followed me, commented to me, and whatever else you can do to connect with someone through social media. You have no idea how much your love and support propelled me through many difficult days. Please don't ever stop reaching out to people who could use a little pick-me-up. The smallest kind gesture can make all the difference.

Resources

So many people from all over the world have supported me in various ways throughout my diagnoses and treatments. Here are a few organizations that have been particularly important to me:

Gilda's Club: The mission of Gilda's Club in Madison is "to ensure that all people impacted by cancer are empowered by knowledge, strengthened by action, and sustained by community." Gilda's Club has locations nationwide.

Website: www.gildasclubmadison.org

Jack & Jill Late Stage Cancer Foundation: The foundation's mission "is treating families to WOW! Experiences®, giving children who will lose their mom or dad to cancer time-out to create indispensable memories as a family . . . while they can."

Website: www.jajf.org

METAvivor: The organization "is dedicated to the specific fight of women and men living with stage IV metastatic breast cancer. At the time of METAvivor's founding, no organization was dedicated to funding research for the disease, and no patient groups were speaking out about the dearth of stage IV cancer research. While more and more people have taken up the cry for more stage IV research, METAvivor remains the sole U.S. organization dedicated to awarding annual stage IV breast cancer research."

Website: www.metavivor.org

About the Authors

HEATHER MCMANAMY

Heather McManamy was a native of West Allis, Wisconsin, and lived in McFarland. She graduated from the University of Wisconsin-Madison and earned a degree in psychology and sociology. She and her husband, Jeff, married in 2006. Their daughter, Brianna, was born in 2011.

After being diagnosed with terminal breast cancer in 2014, Heather retired as a research specialist to focus on cramming a lifetime of memories into her final days with her family. Between countless oncology appointments and chemo treatments, Heather enjoyed living-room dance parties with Brianna, cheering for the Badgers, laughing on the couch with Jeff, posting about her cancer adventures on social media, drinking a glass of wine, and working on projects to ensure Brianna will always know just how much her mommy loves her. Until her last breath, Heather continued to soak in every amazing moment with her wonderful friends and family.

Heather wrote *Cards for Brianna* in just forty-nine days. On the fiftieth day, hours after she had turned in the manuscript to her publisher, Heather passed away peacefully with Jeff at her side. Through *Cards for Brianna,* Heather's love, energy, and essence are still here, growing more and more by the day.

WILLIAM CROYLE

William Croyle is a native of Cleveland, Ohio, and a graduate of Ashland University. He was a journalist at the Cincinnati Enquirer for ten years before becoming a full-time author of inspirational books. He is also the coauthor of *I Choose to Be Happy: A School Shooting Survivor's Triumph Over Tragedy,* with Missy Jenkins Smith; *Angel in the Rubble: The Miraculous Rescue of 9/11's Last Survivor,* with Genelle Guzman-McMillan; *Finding Peace Amid the Chaos: My Escape from Depression and Suicide,* with Tanya Brown; *Expect the Unexpected: Bringing Peace, Healing, and Hope from the Other Side,* with Bill Philipps; and *The Doctor Will See You Now: Recognizing and Treating Endometriosis,* with Tamer Seckin, MD.

William lives in Erlanger, Kentucky, with his wife, Debra, and their three sons. More information on his books is available at www.williamcroyle.com.

If you have enjoyed this book
or it has touched your life in some way,
we'd love to hear from you.

Please send your comments to:
Hallmark Book Feedback
P.O. Box 419034
Mail Drop 100
Kansas City, MO 64141

Or e-mail us at:
booknotes@hallmark.com